Illuminating Life Lessons
Focusing on God

Carol Graves

fullyinfocus@yahoo.com
faacebook: Carol Graves-fullyinfocus

~ Illuminating Life Lessons ~

Copyright © 2019 by Carol Graves

Illuminating Life Lessons
Focusing on God
By Carol Graves
Cover Design by Carol Graves
Printed in the United States of America
Fully in Focus, San Antonio, Texas 78249

ISBN 13: 978-0-9830847-8-5

All rights reserved solely by the author. The author guarantees all contents are original and do not infringe upon the legal rights of any other person or work. No part of this book may be reproduced in any form without the permission of the author.

Bible quotations are taken from:
The Holy Bible. New Living Translation copyright© 1996, 2004, 2007, 2013 by Tyndale House Foundation. Used by permission of Tyndale House Publishers Inc., Carol Stream, Illinois 60188. All rights reserved.

THE HOLY BIBLE, NEW INTERNATIONAL VERSION®, NIV® Copyright © 1973, 1978, 1984, 2011 by Biblica, Inc™ Used by permission. All rights reserved worldwide.

The Message. Copyright © 1993, 1994, 1995, 1996, 2000, 2001, 2002. Used by permission of NavPress Publishing Group.

NEW AMERICAN STANDARD BIBLE®, Copyright © 1960, 1962, 1963, 1968, 1971, 1972, 1973, 1975, 1977, 1995 by The Lockman Foundation. Used by permission

The Holy Bible, English Standard Version. ESV® Permanent Text Edition® (2016). Copyright © 2001 by Crossway Bibles, a publishing ministry of Good News Publishers.

New King James Version®. Copyright © 1982 by Thomas Nelson, Inc. Used by permission. All rights reserved.

~ Illuminating Life Lessons ~

Introduction

We read in **Genesis 1:3-4** *"And God said, "Let there be light," and there was light. And God saw that the light was good. And God separated the light from the darkness."* From the beginning of creation, light has overcome darkness. It wasn't until the 19th century that scientists discovered how light could be produced and the lightbulb was invented. Not only does a light bulb illuminate the darkness in a room, it is used as a symbol to represent the illumination of an idea, a thought, an experience that leads to greater understanding.

Through more than seven decades, God has been teaching me life lessons. Many of these life lessons came as a simple thought, a statement I heard or read, or something I experienced. Some lessons were taught through nature, some through relationships, others through the Bible. Some lessons came easily and were quickly understood. Others required that I walk through pain, sometimes briefly, some for many years, while others are ongoing. I find joy in digging deep to explore exactly what God is saying to me – what He is teaching me.

Each life lesson has challenged me and changed me. They have equipped me to know God in deeper more intimate ways. It is though a light has pierced the darkness bringing illumination to my heart and mind. I am able to see God in new and wonderful ways. As I develop each lesson, I begin to see God's work in my life - His specific work, personal and productive, designed to draw me closer to Him, to know Him more, trust Him more. Each lesson is purposeful, designed accomplish His desire for me. That is to enjoy a relationship with God, to see His glory and experience His peace.

In **Matthew 5:14-16 (ESV),** Jesus taught this: *"You are the light of the world. A city set on a hill cannot be hidden. Nor do people light a lamp and put it under a basket, but on a stand, and it gives light to all in the house. In the same way, let your light shine before others, so that they may see your good works and give glory to your Father who is in heaven."*

The reason I share these life lessons with you is to give you food for thought and to bring glory to God. Perhaps what God has taught me will illuminate your heart and mind to see the God who loves you and cares about you more than you could ever comprehend. My prayer is that you will experience that peace, joy and awe that comes as you discover the illuminating life lessons God has for you.

For God, who said, "Let there be light in the darkness," has made this light shine in our hearts so we could know the glory of God that is seen in the face of Jesus Christ.
2 Corinthians 4:6 (NLT)

~ Illuminating Life Lessons ~

Contents

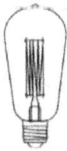

Introduction iii

1. Knowing God 1
2. God is Love 5
3. Discovering the Fullness of God 9
4. God Answers 13
5. Be Specific 17
6. God is Faithful 21
7. Is the Impossible Possible? 25
8. God is at Work 29
9. A Covenant Relationship 33
10. God is Purposeful 37
11. Keep it Simple 41
12. Uncertainty 45
13. God Understands 49
14. God Comforts 53
15. God Wounds but He also Heals 57
16. A New Way of Thinking 61
17. Mother's Day 65
18. Prayer 69
19. Waiting = Trusting.. 73
20. God is a Warrior 77
21. A Day of Remembrance 81
22. God is our Rock 85

23. Not "Why? But "What?"	89
24. According to your Faith	93
25. Declarations	97
26. God Protects	101
27. I AM - Willing	105
28. God is Forgiving	109
29. Forgiveness	113
30. God gives Freedom	117
31. Pulling Weeds	121
32. Choices	125
33. Side Effects	129
34. Grace	133
35. God is Prodigal	137
36. Don't Steal	141
37. Stress	145
38. God is Peace	149
39. Humility	153
40. Contentment	157
41. Blessings	161
42. Fear Not	165
43. Paradox	169
44. Success	173
45. God is Resolute	177
46. God Makes Things New	181
47. Control	185
48. Trust	189
49. Consider the Cost	193
50. The Mediator	197
51. What's in a Name?	201
52. Empty Spaces	207
53. God Finishes	211
54. What is Your Mission?	215

~ Illuminating Life Lessons ~

~ Illuminating Life Lessons ~

Knowing God

Life Lesson: The more I learn about who God is, the more I trust and love Him.

I heard a statement recently that caused me to consider the depth of its meaning. *"You won't love what you don't know."* This turned my thoughts to man's relationship with God. Is it because many don't know God's character that they do not choose to have a relationship with Him? There are some who refuse a relationship with God because they have formed a wrong opinion of Him through limited knowledge. If you were offered to build a relationship with someone who loved you unconditionally, who is forgiving, kind and good – who is faithful and trustworthy, strong and wise and always wants good things for you – how could you turn away? There is so much we need to learn about God's character, and the more you learn, the more you realize that everything about God's character is good.

You may ask, "How do I gain knowledge of God's character?" Think about a person that you know well. How did you come to realize that you could trust them? How did you know that they love you? I am sure if all you did was say hello each day that your relationship would have gone nowhere. Instead you spent time with them and as you observed their actions and interaction with you and others, you learned about their character. You could probably list all the wonderful traits that you discovered leading to that special relationship. In the same way, as we spend time with God, and learn about His character through reading and studying the Scriptures, we begin to know Him more intimately.

More than just knowing who God is, we must share the truth of who God is. I recently saw this profound quote, *"If we don't teach our children who God is, someone else will teach them everything that He isn't."* Our children and grandchildren need to know that God is good and wants good things for them. Sharing what you learn about God's character in your daily life will impact their future relationship with Him. Taking time to build a foundation of faith in your children will help them as they grow older and start making their own choices. If they know the truth of who God is, perhaps they will run TO God rather than away from Him.

God has given me a passion to share the attributes of God with any and all as He gives me the opportunity. This passion has grown through the years but started in a Moms in Prayer group. The mom who led this early group recently shared this statement, *"God kindled our hearts to burn for more of Him. I am grateful."* I, too, am grateful for it has transformed my life. My love for God has grown day by day as I know Him more and more. It has been said that *"the way you define God will always be the way you describe God, but most importantly how you display God."* Although God is beyond our ability to adequately define Him, learning about His attributes gives us a more complete picture of who He is.

I agree with the statement, *"You won't love what you don't know."* The more and more I learn about who God is, the greater is my love for Him. The following is just one passage that helps us "see" who God is.

The LORD is merciful and compassionate, slow to get angry and filled with unfailing love. The LORD is good to everyone. He showers compassion on all his creation. The LORD always keeps his promises; he is gracious in all he does. The LORD helps the fallen and lifts those bent beneath their loads. The eyes of all look to you in hope; you give them their food as they need it. When you open your hand, you satisfy the hunger and thirst of every living thing. The LORD is righteous in everything he does; he is filled with kindness. The LORD is close to all who call on him, yes, to all who call on him in truth. He grants the desires of those who fear him; he hears their cries for help and rescues them. The LORD protects all those who love him, but he destroys the wicked. I will praise the LORD and may everyone on earth bless his holy name forever and ever. Psalms 145:8-9, 13b-21 (NLT)

I have found that the more I focus on who God is, the greater is my faith, my trust, my hope, my peace and my victory.

Let your roots grow down into him, and let your lives be built on him. Then your faith will grow strong in the truth you were taught, and you will overflow with thankfulness.
Colossians 2:7 (NLT)

~ Illuminating Life Lessons ~

God is Love

Life Lesson: I am the object of God's love.

So often we try to define "love." Although the dictionary gives us words that describe love, the true definition of love is simply "God." God is love. In **1 John 4:16b (NLT)** John states, *"God is love, and all who live in love live in God, and God lives in them."*

In **1 Corinthians 13:4-7 (NLT)** we see that God and love are interchangeable. "***God* is patient and kind. *God* is not jealous or boastful or proud or rude. *God* does not demand His own way. *God* is not irritable, and He keeps no record of being wronged. *God* does not rejoice about injustice but rejoices whenever the truth wins out. *God* never gives up, *God* never loses faith, *God* is always hopeful, and *God* endures through every circumstance."**

In his book, *Abiding in Christ,* author Andrew Murray says this about God's love. "Love is not an attribute, but the very essence of His nature, the center around which all His glorious attributes revolve. It is because He is love that He is the Father, and that there is a Son. Love needs an object to give itself away to, in whom it can lose itself, with whom it can make itself one."

We were created to be the object of God's love. What an amazing thought! The nature of His love does not change regardless of the nature of the object of His love. Rejoice in the knowledge that you are the object of God's perfect, unending love!

Consider God's perfect love for you as you read the following scriptures.

Deuteronomy 7:9 (NLT) Understand, therefore, that the LORD your God is indeed God. He is the faithful God who keeps his covenant for a thousand generations and lavishes his unfailing love on those who love him and obey his commands.

Psalm 36:7 (NLT) How precious is your unfailing love, O God! All humanity finds shelter in the shadow of your wings.

Zephaniah 3:17 (NLT) For the LORD your God is living among you. He is a mighty savior. He will take delight in you with gladness. With his love, he will calm all your fears. He will rejoice over you with joyful songs."

John 3:16 (NLT) For this is how God loved the world: He gave his one and only Son, so that everyone who believes in him will not perish but have eternal life.

~ Illuminating Life Lessons ~

Romans 8:39 (NLT) No power in the sky above or in the earth below—indeed, nothing in all creation will ever be able to separate us from the love of God that is revealed in Christ Jesus our Lord.

1 John 4:10 (NLT) This is real love—not that we loved God, but that he loved us and sent his Son as a sacrifice to take away our sins.

1 John 3:1a (NLT) See how very much our Father loves us, for he calls us his children, and that is what we are!

Come along with me as we stroll through the alphabet and ponder all the attributes of God's love.

God's love is accessible, it is boundless, it is compassionate, it defends. God's love encourages, it is faithful, it is full of grace and it heals. God's love is impartial, it brings joy, it knows all and it leads. God's love is merciful, it is always near, it overcomes, it is patient. God's love quiets the troubled soul, it restores, and it saves. God's love transforms, it is unfailing, it is victorious, and it is wise. God's love sees all, like an X-ray. It does not yield to the enemy and God is zealous to let us know how much he loves us.

Oh, how He loves you and me!

And may you have the power to understand, as all God's people should, how wide, how long, how high, and how deep his love is. May you experience the love of Christ, though it is too great to understand fully. Then you will be made complete with all the fullness of life and power that comes from God. Ephesians 3:18-19 (NLT)

~ Illuminating Life Lessons ~

~ Illuminating Life Lessons ~

Discovering the Fullness of God

Life Lesson: When I focus on God it becomes clear that God is enough.

I remember a day when I earnestly prayed, "Lord, fill up the empty spaces in my life!" Through life's experiences, I have come to the realization that we all have those empty spaces. Perhaps the emptiness is revealed in relationships, through disappointment or grief. It may be found in tragedy, illness, loneliness or unfulfilled expectations. Whatever the cause, focusing on the emptiness prevents us from experiencing the peaceful, abundant life that God desires for his children.

All along the journey of life we travel on roads that are sometimes smooth and other times, bumpy. Often, just as we feel that our journey is going well, THUD! We hit a pothole. A pothole is described as a deep hole or pit that is formed due to fatigue of the pavement surface. The worn-down road forms cracks that grow and after a rain they become filled with water that soon causes the pavement to wash away, forming an empty space in the road. The definition of "empty" gives a clear description of a pothole: containing nothing; having nothing in it; having no worth or purpose; useless or unsatisfying.

In life's journey there are times when we become fatigued and worn down and those empty spaces start to appear. Sometimes we dig our own potholes. At other times they come as an unexpected, unwelcome surprise. Just as those who try to fill up potholes in the roads time after time, we may attempt to fill the empty spaces in our lives with things the world offers. It is as though we fill them with water, not understanding that things we try to substitute -- to fill the emptiness -- will fail in time or will not satisfy at all. As we continue to try more and different ways to fill the empty spaces, the vast emptiness only grows greater. We patch them, but they come back. In time we may become so focused on the potholes that we lose sight of the beauty of the journey. The need to resurface -- and maintain -- becomes necessary in order to ensure that the road we travel will result in a safe and peaceful journey.

I have discovered the way to maintain a peaceful life journey is to **keep my focus on God.** Though I still may face obstacles or threats of danger, by shifting my focus from the empty spaces -- the "potholes" of life -- to God, I discover that those empty spaces are filled up with God's fullness and I experience peace. This clear focus brings about joy, inner strength and confidence in God. No longer do I fear what may be ahead or just around the corner of life, for God is with me and He is sufficient and faithful to fill the empty spaces I may face.

God heard my prayer as I asked Him to fill the empty spaces in my life. His answer came clearly as He spoke to my heart and said, *"Focus on me. Become acquainted with who I am. Receive my gift of eternal love and you will find that those empty spaces will become full."* Fullness is defined as having in it all there is space for; rich or abounding; complete. At times we must empty our mind or our heart of anger, bitterness, expectations or disappointments in order to make room for God's fullness. When those thoughts resurface, we must recognize that God wants to fill that emptiness with all that He is. Focusing on the fullness of God has transformed my life journey, causing those empty spaces to lose their power.

What are your empty spaces? Let God fill them up. As you learn more about Him and trust Him, you will find that He is enough. God may reveal some empty spaces in your life of which you were unaware. You may see, and more clearly understand, the empty spaces in the lives of others. Whatever the case, God alone is sufficient to permanently fill and restore all the empty spaces in your life journey.

As you learn to become **fully in focus** of God you will experience the fullness of this promise found in **Isaiah 26:3 (NLT), You will keep in perfect peace all who trust in You – all whose thoughts are fixed (focused) on You.**

~ Illuminating Life Lessons ~

~ Illuminating Life Lessons ~

God Answers

Life Lesson: God hears and answers my every prayer.

Recently I opened a book and on the dedication page was a statement that a prayer was prayed on a specific date that God answered many years later. As I read this I recalled a verse that caused me to question that statement. In **Isaiah 65:24 (NLT)** we read, *"I will answer them before they even call to me. While they are still talking about their needs, I will go ahead and answer their prayers!"* What a thought-provoking verse! God's ways are far beyond my comprehension. God is omniscient. He knows our hearts, our thoughts and every detail of our lives. He knows our present and future needs, our fears, our failures and our victories. Yet even though He is able to provide, to protect, to heal and to meet our every need, we must ask, believe and trust. It has been said that the only prayers God can't answer are the prayers that are not prayed. So, we must ask, but when does God answer?

When someone asks you a question, do you wait until days, weeks, or even years to respond? Usually, we respond immediately. This verse suggests that God answers immediately or even before our prayer is formulated by our mind or spoken by our voice. And if God answers the moment we pray, why must we keep praying the same prayer over and over, waiting for the answer to be revealed?

God's ways are always purposeful. When the disciples asked Jesus to teach them to pray, after teaching them what we refer to as the Lord's Prayer, he told the parable of the friend in need and how his persistence resulted in provision. **(Luke 11:5-10 NLT)** Also, in Luke when teaching the parable of the persistent widow, we read, *"And he told them a parable to the effect that they ought always to pray and not lose heart."* Luke 1:1 (ESV) Jesus was teaching us to ask and keep asking. But why?

I believe that when God hears our prayer, He answers, then sets His plan in place. He starts His perfect work in us drawing us closer to Himself. We sometimes must wait until His answer is revealed, but while we wait there is a work of faith and trust building within us drawing us closer to Him. Whether we receive the answer immediately or we wait, God is asking us to trust in His wisdom and His timing. We must have faith, believing that He is able to do what to us might seem impossible.

One day my grandson was in the car with me and we were on our way to pick up his sister. I mentioned that we might go to his favorite play place for lunch. He immediately asked, "Grandma, are we going there for lunch?" I replied, "We'll see." A few minutes later he said, "Are we going to go to the play place?" I said, "We might." After a few moments he said, "Grandma, just say YES!" Isn't that just like us? We feel that God hasn't answered unless He says yes.

~ Illuminating Life Lessons ~

God responds to our pleas in ways that will bring Him glory and His ways are always for our good. When His answer is revealed, whether it is "yes," "no," "not now," or "I have a better plan," in hindsight, not only do we understand the reason for the period of time between the praying and the revealed answer, we see that His answer is always perfectly timed, in the will of God and brings glory to His Name. So, come boldly to the throne of God. Ask. Believe. Trust. God Answers.

Matthew 6:8b (NLT)...for your Father knows exactly what you need even before you ask him!

Ephesians 3:20 (NLT) Now all glory to God, who is able, through his mighty power at work within us, to accomplish infinitely more than we might ask or think.

Isaiah 65:1 (NLT) The LORD says, "I was ready to respond, but no one asked for help. I was ready to be found, but no one was looking for me. I said, 'Here I am, here I am!' to a nation that did not call on my name.

Psalm 20:6-7 (ESV) Now I know that the LORD saves his anointed; he will answer him from his holy heaven with the saving might of his right hand. Some trust in chariots and some in horses, but we trust in the name of the LORD our God.

> I will praise the LORD at all times. I will constantly speak his praises. I will boast only in the LORD; let all who are helpless take heart. Come, let us tell of the LORD's greatness; let us exalt his name together. I prayed to the LORD, and he answered me. He freed me from all my fears.
> **Psalm 34:1-4 (NLT)**

~ Illuminating Life Lessons ~

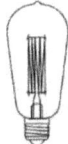

Be Specific

Life Lesson: When I pray specifically, God answers specifically.

When asking a question, I find it difficult to know how to react when responses are vague. For example, if I ask my family, "Would you like chicken or spaghetti?" at times their response is, "Which ever is easiest." I am willing to cook either dish, regardless of the ease of preparation, I just would like to know which they prefer. I am asking a specific question and hoping for a specific answer.

There is an account in the Bible of a time when Jesus was leaving Jericho and Bartimaeus, a blind beggar, was sitting beside the road and heard the noise of a crowd. When he learned that it was Jesus passing by, he began to shout, "Jesus, Son of David, have mercy on me!" Those around him told him to be quiet, but louder and louder he cried out until Jesus stopped and asked that the man be brought to Him. As Bartimaeus came near, Jesus asked, **"What do you want me to do for you?"** Let's stop and think about that for a moment. Do you think Jesus didn't know what the man wanted? Of course, He knew. But He wanted this blind man to be specific. Answering Jesus question, Bartimaeus said, **"Rabbi, I want to see!"** Now Jesus said, **"Go, for your faith has healed you."**

Mark Batterson, author of *The Circle Maker* uses this story to make an important point. He says "We don't get what we want because we don't know what we want. Some prayers are so vague there is no way to know whether God has answered them or not." Some time ago I realized that often as I pray, I ask God to "bless" my child. Although we want God's blessings, exactly what are we asking for? Now I ask God's specific blessing – "Bless my child with Your wisdom as she makes this decision," or "I ask for your blessing of protection when she travels to school." The more you know about God's character, the more faith you have and the more specific your prayers will be – and the more specific your prayers are, the more glory God receives. When we pray specifically and God answers specifically, we can tell others, "God did that!" It affirms our faith and inspires the faith of others. It becomes so exciting!

Corrie Ten Boom said this:
"Any concern too small to be turned into a prayer
is too small to be made into a burden."

Why do we carry these heavy burdens that steal our peace? It has been said that our biggest problem is our small view of God. His Word is filled with promises and He keeps every one of them. When God says, "I will, He does!" So, when you pray, be bold! Ask God specifically for what you need.

~ Illuminating Life Lessons ~

As we pray, however, it is imperative to distinguish between your will and God's will. Every prayer must pass a twofold litmus test: your prayers must be in the will of God and for the glory of God. With confidence, trust and faith, bring your cares and concerns before God, then YIELD those cares and concerns to Him. To yield means to "give up." That is what God wants us to do. He wants us to give up our cares and concerns, hand them over to Him, get out of His way, and let Him do His work. Resist praying ASAP prayers – "Please do it God – As soon as possible." Instead, trust God and start praying ALAT prayers, "As Long As it Takes."

With our focus on who God is, we can have confidence to boldly bring our specific cares and concerns to God, then yield them – give them up to Him. God has promised that He will answer our prayers according to His perfect will, in His perfect time and in a way that will bring Him glory.

"You parents—if your children ask for a loaf of bread, do you give them a stone instead? Or if they ask for a fish, do you give them a snake? Of course not! So if you sinful people know how to give good gifts to your children, how much more will your heavenly Father give good gifts to those who ask him.
Matthew 7:9-11 (NLT)

You faithfully answer our prayers with awesome deeds, O God our savior. You are the hope of everyone on earth.
Psalm 65:5 (NLT)

~ Illuminating Life Lessons ~

God is Faithful

Life Lesson: I can trust in the faithfulness of God.

I enjoy looking up the definition of the attributes of God and observing how perfectly it describes God. The word "faithful" is defined as "constant, loyal, worthy of trust, consistently reliable, adhering firmly and devotedly." Throughout the Bible we see that these descriptions are accurate. In **Hebrews chapter 11** we read a narrative of many who trusted God, though the God given promise was not yet seen. In verse one we read, ***"Faith is the confidence that what we hope for will actually happen; it gives us assurance about things we cannot see."***

In **John chapter six** we read about great multitude of people who followed Jesus because of the signs and wonders they had seen Him perform. Jesus joined His disciples up on the mountain and, looking at the crowd, He knew that they were hungry. He turned to Phillip and asked a question, ***"Where can we buy bread to feed all these people?"*** What must have gone through Phillip's mind? Of course, Jesus knew that the situation looked impossible. Surely there was no human response that would meet the need.

Phillip offered an answer but acknowledged that it would in no way feed the large crowd. The scripture then reads, *"He (Jesus) already had in His mind what He was going to do."* Why, then, do you think Jesus asked the question?

I believe that Jesus was simply trying to test Phillip – to put his heart in a place where he must trust in the faithfulness of God. The provision had already been made. It came about because a little boy was willing to give his lunch to Jesus. This one miraculous act of provision ministered to everyone who had gathered there.

Author, Peggy Joyce Ruth says, *"Faith is not a tool to manipulate God into giving you something you want. Faith is simply the means by which we accept what God has already made available."* In **Isaiah 65:24 (NLT)** we read, *"I will answer them before they even call to me. While they are still talking about their needs, I will go ahead and answer their prayers!"* There is no problem that we face that God has not already solved. Like the little boy in the crowd, we simply must give what we have to Jesus and trust Him to do the rest.

Recently at a church service we sang the hymn *Great is Thy Faithfulness*. As I sang this familiar hymn I began to focus on the words and how they express the ways that God is faithful. The hymn declares that God is unchanging, compassionate and eternal. God is merciful, provider, creator and loving. God is forgiving, present, strong, and the giver of enduring peace. God is the source of blessing and His faithfulness to me is great.

I discovered that this hymn was written by Thomas Chisholm, not as a result of great challenges, but as a testament to God's faithfulness day in and day out regardless of the circumstances. He said, *"I must not fail to record here the unfailing faithfulness of a covenant-keeping God and that He has given me many wonderful displays of His providing care, for which I am filled with astonishing gratefulness."*

There are times when we experience challenges or situations that we do not understand. It seems impossible to see a positive outcome. Yet, the fact that God is faithful is not dependent upon our understanding of Him. Our trust in Him is the key to experiencing His faithfulness. As we trust Him, often in hindsight, we see how God was at work for our good. As His faithfulness is revealed, our faith in Him grows strong.

Today may be a good day or a challenging day for you. Whatever you are experiencing, take time to praise God for His faithfulness. Our trust, hope, confidence and assurance in God's provision rests in the fact that God is faithful.

"All I have needed Thy hand hath provided.
Great is Thy faithfulness, Lord unto me."

The faithful love of the LORD never ends! His mercies never cease. Great is his faithfulness; his mercies begin afresh each morning. I say to myself, "The LORD is my inheritance; therefore, I will hope in him!" Lamentations 3:22-24 (NLT)

~ Illuminating Life Lessons ~

~ Illuminating Life Lessons ~

Is the Impossible Possible?

Life Lesson: With God, nothing is impossible!

With each day, we walk from the known into the unknown. From what is certain to what is uncertain. As a mother, we go through transitions with our children – from infant to toddler, from young child to teenager to adult. With each of these transitions and all the transitions that accompany the changes, we lose more and more control. I have found that most mothers have difficulty with the issue of giving up control. At times our children make choices that we know are not beneficial. We try to protect them but discover that we no longer have control and we must let go, trusting God as He works through each situation.

There are situations in my life that I would change if I could. I realize that I have no control and it seems impossible that things will ever change. At times I try to hold back the thoughts that bring tears. Other times the tears bring relief. Then not once but twice within just a few days God gave me a personal message. First, I heard these words in a prayer, *"But You, God, are able to make the impossible possible."* Soon after this, I received a letter from a friend. In it was a bookmark with a picture that symbolizes my situation and engraved in the leather below the picture were the words, "With God nothing is impossible."

God is so personal – so loving. He knew I needed to be reminded that He knows my situation and that I can trust Him. I recalled the Scriptures that reveal time after time how God intervened in situations that seemed impossible. God established His chosen nation through a son born to Abraham and Sarah in their old age. Joseph, thrown into a pit by his jealous brothers became second in command to Pharaoh in Egypt and rescued his people from famine. Moses led God's people through dry land in the Red Sea as he delivered them from slavery. God gave victory to Joshua and His people causing the walls of Jericho to fall at the mere sound of trumpets and a great shout. Gideon, with only 300 men, caused the enemy to flee by simply breaking clay pots and shouting. As a young boy, David slew a giant with a sling shot and stones. God delivered Daniel unharmed from a den of lions and delivered Shadrach, Meshach and Abednego from a furnace of fire.

I realized that we celebrate the greatest impossibility – a virgin gave birth to a son, Jesus Christ, - God in human flesh. Yet the impossibilities did not stop there. Jesus lived a perfect life and sacrificially fulfilled the justice God required to pay the penalty for the sins of mankind. God so loved mankind and His desire was to restore the relationship He intended from the beginning of creation. That which seemed impossible, God made possible. But there is even more! God claimed victory over sin and death when Jesus raised from the dead. God shows us that He is able to make the impossible possible.

God reminded me through the prayer of my friend and the bookmark that what seems impossible to me, God is able, through His work within any situation, to bring about a result that is beyond anything I can ask or imagine. Now I press on in peace and with hopeful expectation. I choose to walk from the impossible to the possible putting my faith in God who is able. Although the situation has not changed, I pray and wait expectantly for God to do what only He can do.

What impossibility do you face? Is there anything greater than God? Walk with me through this time of transition. Yield all control to God who is able to make the impossible possible!

Now all glory to God, who is able, through his mighty power at work within us, to accomplish infinitely more than we might ask or think. Ephesians 3:20 (NLT)

~ Illuminating Life Lessons ~

God is at Work

Life Lesson: When plans change, consider that God is working out His plan.

In physics, a force is said to do work if, when acting on a body, there is a displacement of the point of application in the direction of the force. Think of that carefully. If we apply this to the spiritual realm, something is accomplished when God, the force, acts upon our spirit, our mind, will or emotion, or our body, and something is displaced or changed in the direction of God's point of application.

Recently I have been privileged to witness the work of God. I got a call asking that the dates of a prayer group I lead needed to be changed to accommodate one of the moms in the group. Just before the meeting on the day she requested, I received a text that this person, whom we agreed to accommodate, would not be attending. "Well," I thought, "that's interesting." A few minutes before I left, I received a call from another mom who told me that she would be bringing a friend with her to our prayer time. This mom, she explained, is a mother of 9 who homeschools her children and was facing surgery the next day for cancer which had reoccurred. God had worked, changing our schedule, to allow us to pray for this mom and encourage her to trust in His faithfulness.

This same week I had interviewed a potential renter for my mother's home. There were concerns about the credit report, so my husband and I sat with the couple to hear their story. After a difficult but productive discussion, we agreed that this couple would be acceptable, and we offered the lease agreement. They were ecstatic declaring that this was a "God thing." Indeed, it was, but not with the outcome we anticipated.

The day arrived to sign the agreement and receive payment. The wife came alone. She asked if she could walk through the house and as she did, her body language gave us pause. She slowly came to the front door and tearfully stated that they would not be able to sign the lease. She explained that because of personal problems she did not have peace about the move. My husband had to leave for an appointment, and I invited her to sit and talk. Having no close family to ask for guidance, she felt alone and unsure. God allowed me to share encouragement and counsel that I had received from His Word as well as through many years of marriage. I was excited to see God's hand at work. He had brought these people into my life, not to rent a house, but to hear from Him.

I am learning that when plans change, I must consider what work God is doing in me or in the people around me. In each of these situations His work resulted in a change of perspective in the lives of those who needed encouragement. It is an exciting adventure to yield to Him in the direction of His force to achieve His eternal purpose.

The scriptures are a record of God's mighty works. We read in **Isaiah 64:8(ESV) But now, O LORD, you are our Father; we are the clay, and you are our potter; we are all the work of your hand.** Picture the potter, carefully molding the clay into a useful vessel, then passing it through the furnace to make it strong. God works in each of our lives, creating unique individuals, allowing the challenges of life to refine us. Then as we allow Him to use us for His purposes, we find fulfillment and joy. As you read the following scriptures, consider the work God is doing in your life and praise Him that His works are designed to accomplish His plan and His plan is perfect.

Deuteronomy 32:4 (NIV) He is the Rock, his works are perfect, and all his ways are just. A faithful God who does no wrong, upright and just is he.

Psalm 66:5 (NIV) Come and see what God has done, how awesome his works in man's behalf!

Isaiah 64:4 (NLT) For since the world began, no ear has heard and no eye has seen a God like you, who works for those who wait for him!

Romans 8:28 (NIV) And we know that in all things God works for the good of those who love him, who have been called according to his purpose.

Ephesians 2:10 (NIV) For we are God's workmanship, created in Christ Jesus to do good works, which God prepared in advance for us to do.

O Sovereign LORD, you have begun to show to your servant Your greatness and Your strong hand. For what god is there in heaven or on earth who can do the deeds and mighty works You do?" Deuteronomy 3:24 (NIV)

A Covenant Relationship

Life Lesson: I can trust that when God says, "I will," He keeps His promises.

I am always excited when I am invited to a wedding. Having two daughters, I have experienced the joy of preparing for the wedding day, then seeing the happiness of the young couple as they start their life together.

I have attended many weddings through the years, and it seems that each one has its unique moments. However, during the wedding ceremony, often the minister instructs the couple that they are entering into a covenant relationship. A covenant relationship is based upon mutual commitments where two or more parties come together to make a contract, agreeing on promises, stipulations, privileges, and responsibilities.

As the bride and groom begin the traditional wedding vows, each is asked a question and the first words they speak are, "I will." Couples promise "to have and to hold, from this day forward, for better, for worse, for richer, for poorer, in sickness and in health, to love and to cherish 'till death do us part." With dreams and expectations of the future I wonder how many couples comprehend what they have promised on that day. One comes to realize the depth of the meaning of these vows over time as challenges and difficulties arise. The covenant relationship is tested and at times, the covenant is broken.

As I thought of these vows, I considered the covenant relationship God has promised to those who enter into a relationship with Him.

"To have and to hold" Psalm 37:23-25 (NLT) The LORD directs the steps of the godly. He delights in every detail of their lives. Though they stumble, they will never fall, for the LORD holds them by the hand.

"from this day forward" Psalm 121:8 (NLT) The LORD keeps watch over you as you come and go, both now and forever.

"for better" Deuteronomy 28:2 (ESV) And all these blessings shall come upon you and overtake you, if you obey the voice of the LORD your God.

"or for worse" Romans 5:6 (NLT) When we were utterly helpless, Christ came at just the right time and died for us sinners.

"for richer" Proverbs 22:4 (NLT) True humility and fear of the LORD lead to riches, honor, and long life.

"for poorer" **Psalm 72:12 (NLT)** He will rescue the poor when they cry to him; he will help the oppressed, who have no one to defend them.

"in sickness" **Psalm 41:3 (NLT)** The LORD nurses them when they are sick and restores them to health.

"and in health" **Isaiah 38:16 (NLT)** Lord, your discipline is good, for it leads to life and health. You restore my health and allow me to live!

"to love and to cherish" **Psalm 36:7 (NLT)** How precious is your unfailing love, O God! All humanity finds shelter in the shadow of your wings.

"till death do us part." **1 Corinthians 15:54-56 (NLT)** Then, when our dying bodies have been transformed into bodies that will never die, this Scripture will be fulfilled: "Death is swallowed up in victory. O death, where is your victory? O death, where is your sting?"

The covenant relationship God offers will never be broken for it is written with the blood of His Son, Jesus Christ. This new covenant brings life, hope and peace between God and man. God promises that this covenant of love will never be removed.

Understand, therefore, that the LORD your God is indeed God. He is the faithful God who keeps his covenant for a thousand generations and lavishes his unfailing love on those who love him and obey his commands. Deuteronomy 7:9 (NLT)

As stated earlier, the covenant relationship requires mutual commitment between two parties. God's Word is filled with "I will" promises.

Isaiah 42:16 (NIV) I will lead the blind by ways they have not known, along unfamiliar paths I will guide them; I will turn the darkness into light before them and make the rough places smooth. These are the things I will do; I will not forsake them.

When God says, "I will!" He does.

> I will praise the LORD and may everyone on earth bless his holy name forever and ever. Psalms 145:21 (NLT)

God is Purposeful

Life Lesson: Commit to the Lord **whatever you do, and He will establish your plans. Proverbs 16:3 (NIV)**

As I sat alone in the room waiting for my Bible study group to arrive, I looked at the clock and it was time to start. I waited, thinking that the weather or other circumstances had caused them to be late. Fifteen minutes later, still no one. Doubts crept into my mind. Is it the study? Is it my leadership? I decided to wait another 15 minutes. Still no one. I waited a few more minutes and started gathering my things to go home. Just as I was about to leave one of the ladies from the group walked into the room. "I need to talk," she said tearfully. After over an hour of listening, sharing and praying we embraced and left. As I walked to my car I smiled and thought how amazing it is that God has a plan and purpose for each and every day. God is so personal. He knows our every need. Even those who were absent were excited to hear how God's purpose for that day was fulfilled. And why should we be surprised? God tells us in **Romans 8:28 (NLT)**

And we know that God causes everything to work together for the good of those who love God and are called according to his purpose for them.

God is purposeful. His purpose is eternal. At times we question, "Why?" When we don't understand or when we see that evil appears to prosper, it is difficult to understand why God would allow such things. We are reminded in **Exodus 9:15-17 (NLT)** when God spoke to Pharaoh, He said, *"By now I could have lifted my hand and struck you and your people with a plague to wipe you off the face of the earth. But I have spared you for a purpose—to show you my power and to spread my fame throughout the earth."* Then in **Proverbs 16:4 (NIV),** we read, *"The LORD works out everything to its proper end—even the wicked for a day of disaster."* While we only see the situations that surround us or directly affect us, God sees eternity. **Proverbs 20:24 (NLT)** says, *"The LORD directs our steps, so why try to understand everything along the way?"*

God allowed me to experience His purpose for that day. It was exciting and filled me with joy. God's love and faithfulness are the foundation of His eternal purpose for our lives. As we trust Him, though our limited vision of eternity may bring about questions, our clear vision of God's purpose brings peace. His purpose is directed to a specific end – that we know Him and have a relationship with Him. God is purposeful.

Psalm 33:11 (NIV) But the plans of the LORD stand firm forever, the purposes of his heart through all generations.

Proverbs 19:21 (NIV) Many are the plans in a person's heart, but it is the LORD's purpose that prevails.

~ Illuminating Life Lessons ~

What a privilege it is to be a part of accomplishing God's purpose. With each day new opportunities come to yield to the purposes of God. All too often, busy with daily tasks I overlook the opportunitles God brings into my day. It could be as simple as talking with a neighbor who needs encouragement or as great as investing time in the life of one who needs to experience the love of God. Even the smallest act of kindness can be the beginning of accomplishing God's eternal purpose. I pray that God will open my eyes to the opportunities to join in His work.

The LORD will fulfill his purpose for me; your steadfast love, O LORD, endures forever. Do not forsake the work of your hands.
Psalm 138:8 (ESV)

~ Illuminating Life Lessons ~

~ Illuminating Life Lessons ~

Keep it Simple

Life Lesson: In the presence of God even my daily tasks can be an act of worship unto Him.

Recently a young mom asked me, "I am so busy all the time just taking care of my family, how can I manage to spend time with God?" In His amazing way, God had already prepared me with the answer. But first, let me share with you the back story. Recently I attended a Bible study and in the video the teacher referred to a book called *The Practice of the Presence of God* by Brother Lawrence. I had not read this book, but because of my passion to know God through the study of His attributes, I decided to order the book. When the book arrived, I saw that it is not a thick, big book with lots of pages, but a small book I thought I could easily read in an hour or so. I was wrong. I have yet to read through this tiny book, for reading it and pondering the thoughts of Brother Lawrence has been both challenging and exciting.

But back to the back story. I started by reading the preface and at the end of the first page there was a short verse. It read,

~ Illuminating Life Lessons ~

"Lord of all pots and pans and things... Make me a saint by getting meals and washing up the plates!" I had assumed that Brother Lawrence must be someone who had a degree in theology, but again I was wrong. Brother Lawrence, according to the preface, was "lowly and unlearned" and spent most of his years as a lay brother working as a cook at a monastery.

When I read the words of the verse, I realized that years ago I had seen these words as part of a poem. When I first saw this poem, I was so moved by the message that I created a plaque that has hung on my kitchen wall for 45 years. But there is more. I had recently started reading the book, *The Purpose Driven Life* by Rick Warren and in it he refers to Brother Lawrence and his book. Coincidence? Absolutely not! God was showing me that He personally knows me, and He put all these things together to show me that He is a living God, working through the details of my life to teach me those things that will bring glory to Him. So, the back story took me from a video to a book to a verse to a plaque to a second book and then came the question from the young mom, "How can I manage to spend time with God?"

God had equipped me with the answer. Using what I had learned from Brother Lawrence I was able to tell this young mom, "Keep it simple." In this little book he states, "Our only business is to love and delight ourselves in God." This humble man who spent his time in a busy kitchen simply desired to "perform all his actions for the love of God." He speaks of having a continual, yet simple conversation with God, recognizing that He is always present with us. That we can praise God, adore Him, love Him and do all that we do "purely for the love of God." He points out that "we ought not to be weary of doing little things for the love of God, who regards not the greatness of the work, but the love with which it is performed." He found no difference in practicing God's presence, whether busy in the kitchen or on his knees in prayer.

This amazing lesson God brought to me personally, not only helped me answer this young mom's question, but also helped me adjust my attitude as I cared for my elderly mom. What a difference it makes when I face frustrations to remember that I am in the presence of God and I can do my daily tasks "for the love of God." I look forward to reading more, but in closing I want to share the poem that hangs on my kitchen wall that surely was penned by Brother Lawrence about 350 years ago. I read the prayer to the young mom and it gave her peace.

My Kitchen Prayer
Lord of all pots and pans and things... since I've no time to be a Saint by doing lovely things or watching late with Thee...or dreaming in the dawn light, or storming Heaven's gates...Make me a Saint by getting meals and washing up the plates. Although I must have Martha's hands, I have a Mary mind...And when I black the boots and shoes, thy sandals, Lord, I find...I think of how they trod the earth each time I scrub the floor...Accept this meditation, Lord, I haven't time for more. Warm all the kitchen with Thy love, and light it with Thy peace...Forgive me all my worrying, and make my grumbling cease...Thou who didst come to give men food in room or by the sea...Accept the grace that I do...
I do it unto Thee.
Amen

So, whether you eat or drink, or whatever you do, do it all for the glory of God. 1 Corinthians 10:31 (NLT)

~ Illuminating Life Lessons ~

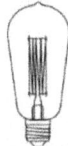

Uncertainty

Life Lesson: Don't look so hard for what you want to see that you overlook the obvious.

Uncertainty is an unwelcome guest in our hearts and minds. Several years ago, I was faced with uncertainty in the life of my son. He was struggling. Everything seemed to be going great, then he contracted meningitis. This led to a chain of events that started a downward spiral. He regained his health, but seemed to be lost, trying to discover his path. As his mother, I was heartbroken for I could not see a future for my son. There were many struggles and my hopes for my son seemed to be dashed day after day. Peace, that rest of heart, mind and spirit, found no place within me.

Because he had little money, my son created handmade gifts that Christmas. The gift he gave me was a framed handwritten scripture that faintly appeared under sponge-painting. I confess, I looked at the art and thought to myself, "The sponge-painting is so dark I can hardly see what it says." I thanked him for his thoughtful gift and hung it on the wall. As I looked at it sometime later, I realized that God had sent me a special message. The scripture, almost hidden under the sponge-painting, were words spoken by God and delivered by Jeremiah to God's people who had been exiled and were in Babylonian captivity. God said to them, **"For I know the plans I have for you to give you a future and hope."** *Jeremiah 29:11*

God showed me that even though the words seemed hidden and I could not see them clearly, the fact remained that they were there. As I thought about that truth, I understood God's special message to me. Although I could not see a future for my son, although he seemed to be in captivity, the fact remained that God had a plan, a purpose, a future – and this gave me hope. **Proverbs 20:24 (NLT)** states, **"The Lord directs our steps, so why try to understand everything along the way?"** When I first read this verse, I had to pause and think. It became clear that the key to this verse is stated at the beginning. **"The Lord directs our steps..."**

The inner turmoil I was experiencing was actually a result of trying to solve the difficulties myself – trying to chart my son's path. I was not trusting God's Word that He had a plan and purpose for my son. Only when I "gave up" and placed my son's future in the hands of God did I experience peace. God's plan for my son was quite different than I had ever imagined. But he is happy, productive and following God's leadership. By understanding that Sovereign God establishes our plans, and through trusting in His goodness, His love, His faithfulness, and all that He is, I experience the "peace that passes all understanding."

~ Illuminating Life Lessons ~

Before time began, God established His plans for us and sealed them with an eternal covenant of love. Often those plans are obvious, but we look so hard for what we want to see that we overlook the obvious. Because we seek plans of our own, we become blind to what God has planned. As we focus on God, He will "establish the work" of our hands. All glory to God who establishes an eternal peace even in times of uncertainty.

May the favor of the Lord our God rest on us; establish the work of our hands for us—yes, establish the work of our hands. Psalm 90:17 (NIV)

~ Illuminating Life Lessons ~

God Understands

Life Lesson: Our situation may look different from God's point of view.

To put it simply, there are many things we do not understand. The unexpected and unexplained death of a loved one. A family member who walks away from family relationships. Watching a person slip away, losing all remembrance and ability to reason. A job not offered to the one who is most qualified. Surely those things that seem beyond understanding are coming to your mind right now. Some of these things weigh heavily upon our hearts. They bring out emotions that express the deepness of our lack of understanding – frustration, anger, sadness, fear. We find ourselves desperately striving to "figure things out" which only enhances these emotions. In **Ecclesiastes 11:5 (NLT)**, we read, *"Just as you cannot understand the path of the wind or the mystery of a tiny baby growing in its mother's womb, so you cannot understand the activity of God, who does all things."* In this passage God is telling us that regardless of the circumstance, God is at work and God understands.

All too often we become so anxious to unravel the mysteries of life that these "things" become our focus. We ponder or worry, trying to find the answers we so desperately seek. We are filled with questions and doubts arise. Without realizing it our search can lead us into a trap and these "things" can control our thoughts. The enemy now has fertile ground to grow bitterness and fear.

How do we know God understands? When He took on human form, He experienced these "things" personally. He experienced homelessness, hunger and grief. He was betrayed, tempted and abandoned. He knew suffering, pain, fear and desperation. He humbled himself and was obedient to God's purpose.

I am learning that some of these "things" that God allows in our lives are not about us at all. They are God at work through us, perhaps intending to show someone else His power, His comfort, His redemption, His love. Once again, it causes us to trust that He has a much greater perspective. He sees the big picture in completion. We only see the few brush strokes of our lives. God is asking us to trust Him, even when we can't "figure things out." God's Word assures us that He is working all things for our good.

"My thoughts are nothing like your thoughts," says the LORD. And my ways are far beyond anything you could imagine. For just as the heavens are higher than the earth, so my ways are higher than your ways and my thoughts higher than your thoughts." Isaiah 55:8-9 (NLT)

Yes, there are those "things" we may never understand. But God is asking us to love Him above all the "things" that we do not understand. He is asking us to be obedient and give these "things" up to Him. God tells us in His Word that He knows, and He understands – the frustration, the anger, the sadness and the fear. We must understand that God's perspective is much greater than ours. He asks that we trust Him that He will work out those things we do not understand for our good.

> **So then, since we have a great High Priest who has entered heaven, Jesus the Son of God, let us hold firmly to what we believe. This High Priest of ours understands our weaknesses, for he faced all of the same testings we do, yet he did not sin. So let us come boldly to the throne of our gracious God. There we will receive his mercy, and we will find grace to help us when we need it most. Hebrews 4:14-16 (NLT)**

~ Illuminating Life Lessons ~

God Comforts

Life Lesson: In times of despair, God in many ways will personally provide comfort and peace.

Psalm 10:17 (NLT) *LORD, you know the hopes of the helpless. Surely you will hear their cries and comfort them.* This scripture tells us that God knows and understands our situation. It states that **surely,** which means without a doubt, unquestionably, certainly, God will hear our cries and encourage, strengthen, console, calm or inspire with hope those who cry out to Him. Whatever situation brings us to a place of sadness, despair or hopelessness, in many ways God provides the comfort that will bring us to a place of peace.

I have experienced God's comfort in tangible ways. When my mother's health was declining rapidly, we moved her to a home care facility where kind and experienced caregivers gave her the 24-hour personal care she needed. The process of clearing out her home in order to provide needed finances was overwhelming. We had a big garage sale and at the end of the day, her home that was the source of so many special memories was empty.

I woke up the next morning tearful as I considered all that had transpired over the past several weeks. I believe God prompted me to recall some of the ways He personally gave me comfort. Each time we sold a piece of furniture, the new owners commented how delighted they were to place it in their home. The dining room furniture would now be the table where a new family would gather for Thanksgiving dinner just as our family had done for so many years. There was a kitchen table where I had sat with my mother and the chairs that badly needed reupholstered due to the cat using them as a scratching post. A young college boy found the set to be affordable on his limited budget and he looked forward to the challenge of fixing them. The couch and loveseat upholstered in a fabric with pastel flowers that we thought would never sell was purchased by a little lady who was delighted with its beauty.

As we closed the garage sale, of course there were many things that remained. I realized that the jobs that would have given me great sadness had been accomplished by those who had come to help that day. The clothes my mom had worn were boxed up by my sister-in-law. The knick-knacks were packed carefully by my dear friend. Others sent messages that they were praying for me. I was so very thankful for these simple things that brought me great comfort.

God's Word declares, **"As a mother comforts her child, so will I comfort you."** Isaiah 66:13a (NIV). My daughter was there to help as well and with her was my baby granddaughter. Just holding that baby close was another source of comfort. God was aware of my needs and He provided mercy and grace throughout the day.

God tells us in His Word, *"All praise to God, the Father of our Lord Jesus Christ. God is our merciful Father and the source of all comfort. He comforts us in all our troubles so that we can comfort others. When they are troubled, we will be able to give them the same comfort God has given us.*
2 Corinthians 1:3-4 (NLT)

I am now more aware that a simple word of encouragement, an act of kindness, a prayer or even just our physical presence can minister comfort. As we have been comforted, let us be aware of and available to those among us who are in need of God's comfort.

Now may our Lord Jesus Christ himself and God our Father, who loved us and by his grace gave us eternal comfort and a wonderful hope, comfort you and strengthen you in every good thing you do and say. 2 Thessalonians 2:16- (NLT)

~ Illuminating Life Lessons ~

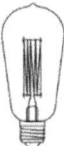

God Wounds but He also Heals

Life Lesson: Brokenness allows us to see the greatness of God.

There are times when God gives us tests that are just little pop quizzes, but on a rare icy day in San Antonio I experienced something that was more like the SAT! As we woke up that morning, we saw that in the night there had been a light snowfall and a somewhat significant ice storm. Our nephew, whom we had not seen for a few years, had spent the night with us. As we prepared to leave for work that morning, my husband had gone into the garage to get an ice scraper. I was in the kitchen and heard my husband calling. I stepped into the garage and saw the garage door was open. Then I saw my husband on the driveway, flat on his back crying out in pain. As he stepped onto the driveway, one small patch of black ice had caused one foot to slip while the other stayed planted. My husband said, "I think I have broken my foot."

I immediately called 911 and rushed to get my nephew for help. It was freezing cold and my husband could not get up. He said,

"Just leave me here." I knew that he could be going into shock and that leaving him on the cold driveway was not an option, but I had no idea how to get him into the house. Our nephew asked if we had a tarp and I quickly found one. Hoping to avoid a fall ourselves we placed the tarp on the driveway and helped my husband painfully roll onto the tarp, then we dragged him into the garage. I remembered that we had some crutches in the storage closet and, with the crutches, we helped him make his way onto the couch where we waited for the ambulance.

In those few minutes that seemed like an eternity, God had demonstrated His provision. Not by coincidence our nephew who lived overseas was with us that day and I was not alone. God gave us wisdom to quickly find solutions to the obstacles we faced. Although the adrenalin was pumping, I was not fearful for God filled me with His peace. God's presence assured me that He was in control and He would see us through this time of challenges.

While we waited in the emergency room for the results of the X-ray, we were calm and I said, "Just think, six months from now we will look back at this and laugh." Little did I know what was ahead. Six months would have been the pop quiz. God was getting us ready for the SAT. The emergency room doctor came with the results of the X-ray. He told us that both bones in my husband's leg were broken, and it looked like a bunch of jumbled puzzle pieces. Then, after being admitted to the hospital, the orthopedic doctor came in and his first words were, "If you were a horse…."

The journey lasted almost four years with repeated complications. There were several infections resulting from the metal plates and screws which required surgeries to be removed – one by one. After almost two years, the doctor said that the weight bearing bone had several areas of non-union and that a bone graft would be necessary. Things seemed to be getting worse, not better. And things did get worse when the bone graft failed resulting in more infection and it had to be removed.

Each time they operated, they had to make wounds on his leg so that the infection could be cleaned out and for the bones to be secured with hardware. The last thing they did after each surgery was to carefully bandage the wounds they had caused so that his leg could heal. It was sometime later that I read the following verse: **Job 5:18 (NLT) For *though he wounds, he also bandages. He strikes, but his hands also heal.***

I had never considered that God causes wounds. After reading this verse and because of the experience we had gone through with my husband's broken leg, I realized that, just like the surgeons, God only causes wounds that will bring about healing. The wounds we suffer at His hand He will bandage with His love and heal with His forgiveness. When we are healed, we are whole, new and better than before. Not unlike those broken bones, God allows brokenness to bring us to a place where we no longer trust in ourselves, but trust in God. It changes our perspective.

In the book of Job, we read the account of a man who is wealthy and respected. He is healthy, has a large family and a lives a comfortable lifestyle. Suddenly, and seemingly without cause, Job loses everything – his health, his family, his possessions and his friends. Job chapter 17 paints a vivid picture of one who is broken.

Although Job did not understand why God allowed such suffering, he endured because his life was built upon faith in God. Job discovered at his lowest point that God alone was enough. When all else is stripped away, we can see God more clearly. In **Job 42:5-6 (NIV)**, Job humbly speaks these words: ***"My ears had heard of you but now my eyes have seen you. Therefore, I despise myself and repent in dust and ashes."*** It was then that God restored Job's health, his wealth and his family with even more than he had before.

After almost four years and 12 surgeries, as I look back I see that God met our every need during our time of testing. He showed us His compassion as he brought alongside prayer warriors who continued to pray for healing. He provided financially. He provided encouragement as friends brought meals, visited and called. Most importantly, with His healing power He spared my husband's leg and his life. He provided as He promises a "peace that passes all understanding." God had prepared me to trust Him through this test as I learned to keep my focus on Him.

Brokenness is not something we desire, yet often when we look back, we discover that those times when we are broken are the times when we rely most on God. In hindsight we can see that those times have given us new insight and strength and we can see that there are good reasons for at least some of the tragedy and pain in life. Perhaps from God's perspective, there are good reasons for all of them.

> **The LORD is close to the brokenhearted; he rescues those whose spirits are crushed. Psalms 34:18 (NLT)**
> **He heals the brokenhearted and bandages their wounds.**
> **Psalms 147:3 (NLT)**

A New Way of Thinking

Life Lesson: Life's greatest blessing is experiencing the presence of God.

Life is filled with trials. Life is filled with blessings. As we travel through life, we are faced with all sorts of experiences. How we process these experiences determines our outlook upon the journey. In **Romans 12:2a (NLT)** we are given a challenge. ***"Don't copy the behavior and customs of this world, but let God transform you into a new person by changing the way you think."*** As I read this verse I began to consider, "What exactly is a blessing or a trial?"

In general, when things are going smoothly in our lives, we consider these to be times of blessing. When we face difficulties or challenges, often we consider these times as trials. But what if the difficulties that we face are the times of blessing and the times when things are going smoothly are the times of trial? As I began to explore these thoughts, God showed me a new way of thinking.

Some ask, "Why does God allow the 'trials' of life?" or "How could a loving God allow these things to happen?" Consider this – when is it that we call out to God and most strongly seek and experience His presence? Is it during the times of blessing or the times of trial? Could it be that God wants us to experience the fullness of His presence so deeply that He allows these 'trials' in order to draw us close to Him? We seek His protection, His provision and His comforting presence. God in turn pours out His peace. What is the greatest blessing? Isn't it when we are closest to God experiencing His presence?

You may question, "How do the blessings become the trials?" The first definition of "trial" is "the act of testing." In **Luke 8:13-14 (ESV),** Jesus is teaching the parable of the seeds when He speaks of a time of testing and falling away. "***And the ones on the rock are those who, when they hear the word, receive it with joy. But these have no root; they believe for a while, and in time of testing fall away. And as for what fell among the thorns, they are those who hear, but as they go on their way they are choked by the cares and riches and pleasures of life, and their fruit does not mature.***" Could it be that the times of blessing are a time of testing - testing our relationship, our faith and trust in God? During these good times, do we draw closer to God, focusing on Him or do we tend to become complacent focusing more on the 'things' that we hope will make us feel happy?

When difficult times come, try a new way of thinking. God wants to bless you with an awareness of His presence and power. God will prove Himself to be sufficient to meet your every need. He is ready and able to help you. He loves you. As you look to Him, you will experience the blessing of God's presence resulting in hope and peace.

~ Illuminating Life Lessons ~

Then, when all is well, get ready for the trial that will follow. Will you continue to focus on your relationship with God, growing and maturing in your faith? The things of the world may make us feel happy, but happiness is dependent upon our circumstances. True peace, joy and fulfillment can be found in God alone. He is the One who is faithful, the One who is sufficient, and the One who longs to have fellowship with you.

Are you experiencing a time of blessing or a time of trial? Try a new way of thinking. What once was considered a "trial" will lose its power and become a blessing as you experience the presence of God. And the times of blessing will give you the opportunity to share God's love and grace to those who might need to experience a new way of thinking.

"Consider it pure joy, my brothers and sisters, whenever you face trials of many kinds, because you know that the testing of your faith produces perseverance." James 1:2-3 (NIV)

"My thoughts are nothing like your thoughts," says the LORD. "And my ways are far beyond anything you could imagine. For just as the heavens are higher than the earth, so my ways are higher than your ways and my thoughts higher than your thoughts." Isaiah 55:8-9(NLT)

~ Illuminating Life Lessons ~

Mother's Day

Life Lesson: The memories I make with my children and grandchildren, and the prayers I pray for them will be the most valuable legacy I can leave.

Within the same year I experienced the joy of welcoming a new granddaughter and the sorrow of saying an earthly good-by to my mother. Each year as we celebrate Mother's Day it is a time of sharing fond memories of my mother and anticipating the joy of creating new memories with my little granddaughter.

Often my children ask, "What would you like for Mother's Day?" I now know exactly how I will answer that question. I want to create memories. I want to spend time with my daughters and grandchildren, experiencing new adventures with them. Times when we enjoy conversations about motherhood and times when we share the joy of seeing their children grow and develop. I want to make memories of sharing recipes, teaching my granddaughters to bake, playing board games that make us laugh. I want our families to share holidays together and grow close as we create new memories. That is what I want. Nothing that has a price tag. Just memories that are priceless.

I realize now that my mother is gone that there are so many questions I wish I had asked her. There are so many stories I heard several times that I would love to hear again. Still other stories I would like to hear that will forever remain untold. I have learned the value of communication. I want to establish a legacy that will be a sweet memory for my children.

More than anything else I hope that each of my children and grandchildren will remember that I prayed for them. That is the priceless gift I give to them. I am reminded of a poem by an unknown author that remains my favorite. It has no title – just a simple message.

You may have riches and wealth untold,
Crowns of jewels and coffers of gold,
But richer than I you will never be –
I have a mother
Who prays for me.

The following is a quote attributed to Abraham Lincoln: *"I remember my mother's prayers and they have always followed me. They have clung to me all my life."*

Although our memories may fade with time, our prayers remain for eternity.
"And when he took the scroll, the four living beings and the twenty-four elders fell down before the Lamb. Each one had a harp, and they held gold bowls filled with incense, which are the prayers of God's people." Revelation 5:8 (NLT)

~ Illuminating Life Lessons ~

May you enjoy Mother's Day whether you honor your mother or you are honored by your children. May you create memories that will be treasured for generations to come.

But watch out! Be careful never to forget what you yourself have seen. Do not let these memories escape from your mind as long as you live! And be sure to pass them on to your children and grandchildren. Deuteronomy 4:9 (NLT)

~ Illuminating Life Lessons ~

Prayer

Life Lesson: The prayers I pray for my children and grandchildren will shape the lives of the generations to come.

As I was going through my mother's things, I found a little folded piece of torn brown paper. I could see that it had handwriting on it, so I unfolded it and found a handwritten prayer, penned by my great grandmother. As I pray for my grandchildren, I often wonder if my grandparents, great grandparents or others of my ancestors prayed for me. I think they did.

In his book, *Praying Circles Around Your Children*, Mark Batterson writes this: "Prayer turns ordinary parents into prophets who shape the destinies of their children, grandchildren and every generation that follows." As a 24-year member of the Moms in Prayer ministry, I have seen God's hand at work in response to the prayers I have prayed for my children and grandchildren as well as for many others.

As we pray, we ask for many things, but I have found that if I first focus on who God is and praise Him, my perspective changes. I praise Him, not for what He has done, but for who He is, focusing on His attributes. I recognize that His character is always loving and good. I am learning that this is the most important part of my prayer for it causes me to focus on the One who created me, who loves me, who is wise and strong. I then ask the Holy Spirit to reveal any sin I need to confess. I quietly listen and confess any act or thought that offends God. After receiving His forgiveness, I acknowledge and thank God for the ways I have seen Him answer prayers and how He continues to bless me as He works in my life. This changes my focus from my needs to the One who is able to meet my needs. Now, without hesitation, I am ready to place my cares and concerns in the hands of God and trust in His faithfulness. I find that praying God's Word gives me the assurance that I am praying according to the will of God and in a way that will bring HIm glory.

A verse I pray for my grandchildren is found in **Joshua 22:5b (NLT).** I speak their names as I pray.

"Love the Lord your God, _____, walk in all his ways, obey his commands, hold firmly to him, _____, and serve him with all your heart and all your soul."

God encourages us in His Word to, **"Never stop praying."** **1 Thessalonians 5:17 (NLT)** Oswald Chambers said, *"The prayer of the feeblest saint on earth who lives in the spirit and keeps right with God is a terror to Satan. The very powers of darkness are paralyzed by prayer. No wonder Satan tries to keep our minds fussy in active work till we cannot think in prayer."*

And in **Philippians 4:6-7(NLT)** we are encouraged, *"Don't worry about anything; instead, pray about everything. Tell God what you need and thank him for all he has done. Then you will experience God's peace, which exceeds anything we can understand. His peace will guard your hearts and minds as you live in Christ Jesus."* I encourage you to experience the power of prayer. To *"Give all your worries and cares to God, for he cares about you."* 1 Peter 5:7 (NLT)

My great grandmother and her husband claimed a homestead in the Old Oklahoma land run in 1889. I cannot imagine the challenges she faced as she raised her family. This little prayer I found suggests that she trusted God and that prayer was an important part of her life. I don't know if it is something she copied or if it came from her heart, but I want to share it with you. I thank God for preserving it for me to see.

Prayer for Health

Oh, gracious Father, Bless my mind and keep my body well
that I may glorify your name and constantly excel.
Bestow on me the wisdom and the courage that I need to give
a good example by my every word and deed.
Allow me all the human strength and health of limb and heart
that I must have to do my best in every daily art.
Because I want to serve You well as long as I am here and
carry out successfully a virtuous career,
O gracious Father favor me with mind and body sound, to help
me earn a humble place where peace and joy abound.

Fern Nichols, founder of Moms in Prayer International, writes this, "God answering our prayers will change the course of history! Little did I realize that ordinary moms, releasing God's power through prayer would birth a worldwide prayer movement. Imagine what God could do with an entire generation of prayed for children! Prayer is the greatest legacy we can leave our children."

The earnest prayer of a righteous person has great power and produces wonderful results. James 5:16b (NLT)

~ Illuminating Life Lessons ~

Waiting = Trusting

Life Lesson: God's uses the "waiting room" to give us opportunities to trust Him, for His timing is always perfect.

Why is God never in a hurry? Hint - the answer to this riddle is both a test and a promise.

"Are we there yet?" I remember traveling with my daughter and grandchildren through west Texas one spring to a destination over seven hours away. There was not much to see along the road except hundreds of windmills dotted throughout the fields. Several times my three-year-old grandson asked, "When will we get there?" The concept of a trip taking several hours was unfamiliar to this little one who was used to living in the city. After a nap, he awoke and looked out at the same scenery he had seen earlier and calmly said, "Looks like this is gonna take a while."

The impatient child who wants to quickly reach the final destination of a journey often repeatedly asks, "Are we there yet?" Over and over they ask, never satisfied with any answer other than, "Yes, we are here!" All too often this is the approach we take in our prayer life. There are times when we wait for days, months or even years to see God's answer to our prayers. We must realize that even though we do not see the answer immediately, we must trust that God is at work. We read in ***Isaiah 64:4 (NLT) For since the world began, no ear has heard and no eye has seen a God like you, who works for those who wait for him!***

And there is the problem. We are in a hurry. As the definition of "hurry" describes, we hastily move about, sometimes carelessly and recklessly. We want things done rapidly. We want solutions and answers that will make us feel comfortable. We don't like to wait! To wait is "to stay in a place or remain in readiness or in anticipation until something expected happens." Rather than waiting, we tend to take things into our own hands. The results are not always what we hoped for.

God does not hurry. He teaches us to wait.

It is not that God takes pleasure in torturing us by holding back His answers to our prayers. It is simply that His answers are perfectly timed according to His perfect purpose. To wait while trusting God is to remain in readiness or in anticipation until we see His finished work.

Are you in God's waiting room? Are there prayers you have prayed for days, months, even years that you have not seen answered? The scriptures are clear, that when we wait on God, He will be faithful to act, and He wants good things for us. Our

~ Illuminating Life Lessons ~

timetable may not be the same as His, but we can trust that He will not act in haste. His answers are perfectly timed. It is in the waiting room that our faith can grow as we wait in expectation for His answer. It is there that we can say to Him, "I trust you." As you pray and wait for God, find hope in Him, knowing that He will not act hastily or too quickly, but with perfect timing to bless you with what is best.

The story of Abraham is found in **Genesis 12:1-25:18**. At the age of 75, God spoke to Abraham and promised to make his descendants into a great nation. It was not until he was 99 years old that God confirmed that Sarah, Abraham's 90-year-old wife, would give birth to a son. In Paul's letter to the Romans, he referred to Abraham as one who waited and trusted God. **Romans 4:18-21(NLT)** *Even when there was no reason for hope, Abraham kept hoping—believing that he would become the father of many nations. For God had said to him, "That's how many descendants you will have!" And Abraham's faith did not weaken, even though, at about 100 years of age, he figured his body was as good as dead—and so was Sarah's womb. Abraham never wavered in believing God's promise. In fact, his faith grew stronger, and in this he brought glory to God. He was fully convinced that God is able to do whatever he promises.*

Now, did you find the answer to the riddle? God is never in a hurry because He is always on time. The test – will you trust Him? The promise – He is always on time.

Yet I am confident I will see the LORD's goodness while I am here in the land of the living. Wait patiently for the LORD. Be brave and courageous. Yes, wait patiently for the LORD.
Psalm 27:13-14 (NLT)

~ Illuminating Life Lessons ~

~ Illuminating Life Lessons ~

God is a Warrior

Life Lesson: God asks me to stand firm, trusting Him while He fights the battle.

Some thoughts I find so interesting, I must share them. Consider this: *"You cannot declare victory unless there is a battle."* Victory, the very thing we seek, requires that we experience a battle in order to attain it. Throughout life we engage in battles of many kinds. As I have engaged in life's battles, I have learned that my skills are quite lacking. Many times, these battles have ended in defeat and despair. But God is teaching me that I can declare victory and He has provided all that I need to defeat the enemy.

Throughout the Old Testament there are many references to mighty warriors. They used various weapons and strategies as they fought, but one factor remained clear. As found in **Joshua 11:8 (NLT)**, the scriptures state over and over again, *"And the Lord gave them victory over their enemies."* **2 Corinthians 10:3-4 (NIV)** explains, *"For though we live in the world, we do not wage war as the world does. The weapons we fight with are*

not the weapons of the world. On the contrary, they have divine power to demolish strongholds."

God has equipped us with special armor as we face the enemy. As described in **Ephesians 6:14-17 (NIV)**, our armor includes **the belt of truth, the breastplate of righteousness, feet fitted with the gospel of peace, the shield of faith, the helmet of salvation and the sword of the Spirit, which is the word of God.** As I considered the individual pieces of armor, I realized that all except one are defensive, with a purpose to protect us. The only offensive weapon is God's Word.

Looking closer, I realized that each of the pieces of armor have been given to us as gifts. God gave Jesus who is the Way, the Truth and the Life and He has given us His Word which is truth. We are offered the gift of salvation as we exercise the gift of faith and we are robed in God's righteousness. Jesus offers the gift of peace as He says, *"My peace I give you."* With these gifts God has prepared us for battle, but He is the mighty warrior. **Ephesians 6:10-11,18a (NIV)** tells us *"Finally, be strong in the Lord and in His mighty power. Put on the full armor of God, so that you can take your stand against the devil's schemes... Pray in the Spirit at all times and on every occasion."* Isn't it interesting that we are not instructed to fight? We are instructed only to stand firm and pray.

When I am in the midst of life's battles, I am learning that my efforts fall short of the power of God. Without yielding to the enemy I declare out loud one of my favorite verses from **Exodus 14:14 (NLT)**, *"The LORD himself will fight for you. Just stay calm."* As I acknowledge that only through God's power I will gain victory, I cease striving and remain calm. God is never defeated.

It is interesting that there are many references of great battles in the Old Testament, but few in the New Testament. Why? Because, as He died on the cross, Jesus declared, *"It is finished."* The battle against sin and death is over. When you find yourself in the midst of a battle and the enemy is gaining ground, put on the armor that God has provided to defend you, speak God's Word and remember that God is our mighty warrior and even against the schemes of Satan, victory has been won!

The LORD **is my strength and my song; he has given me victory. This is my God, and I will praise him—my father's God, and I will exalt him! The L**ORD **is a warrior; Yahweh is his name!**
Exodus 15:2-3 (NLT)

~ Illuminating Life Lessons ~

~ Illuminating Life Lessons ~

A Day of Remembrance

Life Lesson: God promises to protect those who love and trust Him.

Memorial Day is a federal holiday in the United States for remembering the people who died while serving in the country's armed forces. This day, originally called Decoration Day, was established in 1868 when, after the Civil War, Union veterans established it as a time for the nation to decorate the graves of the Union war dead with flowers. Later, the day was extended to honor all Americans who died while in military service.

As a child, I remember Memorial Day as a time of family reunion. We would enjoy a pot-luck lunch after visiting and laying flowers on the graves of family. Earlier in the morning the people in our small community gathered around the flagpole that stood at the entrance to the town. The flag was raised to half-mast as taps was played on a trumpet. Many of those present had served in World War II. They had experienced the terrors of war and most kept their stories unspoken. One of the few stories my father shared was an experience that could have altered the lives of our family had it not been for God's protection.

On a cold dark night my father and another soldier were transporting men through enemy territory. They knew the area was filled with land mines. They loaded their passengers and took the driver's seat in the military Jeep. My father was to be in the second Jeep carefully following in the tracks of the first to lessen the chance of hitting a mine. The soldier designated to drive the first Jeep was extremely frightened. My father volunteered to take the lead and started across the field. It was winter and the ground was frozen. As he cautiously drove across the field, although his vehicle did not break through the frozen ground, the second vehicle, following in his tracks was just heavy enough to break through and detonate a land mine. My father was safe. Those in the second Jeep perished.

I think of that story often, realizing that had my father not made the decision to take the lead, I would never have been born. God's protection preserved His purpose for our family. I grieve for the families of those in that second Jeep and honor the memory of their loved ones.

Psalms 91 is the passage that my father read over and over as he slowly crossed Europe for two years facing the enemy. I can only imagine how he clung to God's promise of protection as he drove a half track onto the beach on D-Day 3 and later fought in the Battle of the Bulge.

However, as we read **Psalms 91**, we find that God's promise of protection is conditional. In verse 1 we read, *"**He who dwells in the shelter of the Most High will abide in the shadow of the***

~ Illuminating Life Lessons ~

Almighty. To dwell means to live in; to be settled; to stay; to keep the attention directed upon. Verse 2 continues, *I will say to the Lord, "My refuge and my fortress, My God, in whom I trust!"* In verse 14a we read, *"Because he has loved Me, therefore I will deliver him."* This passage does not promise that we will not face dangers and difficulties, but that He will deliver us through them. It declares that God's promises of protection are in place when we keep our attention directed upon God, and when we trust Him and love Him.

On Memorial Day, let us remember with honor and gratitude those who have died as they served us, protecting our freedom and our nation. Let us pray for their families that God will give them peace. Let us pray Psalm 91 over those who are now engaged in the dangers of war. And let us experience God's promise of protection as we dwell in the shelter of the Most High, giving God our trust and our love.

> **Lord, don't hold back your tender mercies from me. Let your unfailing love and faithfulness always protect me.**
> **Psalm 40:11 (NLT)**

The following poem was written by my brother and his son in honor of our father, Ernest Reynolds, Jr. He shipped out just two weeks after my brother was born. His fellow soldiers called him "Pops."

MEMORIAL DAY

DUSK IS GONE FIRST LIGHT IS NEAR,
THE DAY HAS COME AT LAST.
MEMORIAL DAY THE BUGLES PLAY,
THE FLAGS ARE FLOWN HALF-MAST.
THE GUNS ARE FIRED, THE COLORS RETIRED,
FRIENDS AND LOVED ONES SEE
THE EPITAPH UPON THE GRAVES.
THEY DIED FOR YOU AND ME.

FLOWERS ARE PLACED, THE WREATHS ARE LAID,
AN HONOR GUARD PLAYS TAPS ONCE MORE.
AGAINST A DARKENED PURPLE SKY, WE SEE AN EAGLE SOAR.
AS THE DAY FADES INTO DUSK AND LIGHT FADES INTO NIGHT,
THOSE WHO FOUGHT FOR LIBERTY,
AND THOSE WHO FOUGHT FOR RIGHT LAY GENTLY NOW,
YET EVEN STILL THEIR MEMORIES WE EMBRACE.
WHAT WOULD WE NOT GIVE AGAIN TO ONLY SEE THEIR FACE.

IF WE LISTEN CLOSELY TO THE BREEZE,
WE CAN HEAR THE SOLDIERS SAY,
"AS YOU ENJOY YOUR FREEDOM,
REMEMBER ME – MEMORIAL DAY."

~ Illuminating Life Lessons ~

God is our Rock

Life Lesson: Times change, life brings changes, but God is our Rock where we will not be shaken.

When my husband and I prepared to celebrate our 50th wedding anniversary we decided to have our picture taken. As we posed for the photographer, she asked us, "What is the key to such a lasting relationship?" I saw this as an opportunity to share with this young woman not only about my relationship with my husband, but also my relationship with God. I replied, "Communication, unconditional love, but most of all building our marriage upon a foundation of faith in God." We continued to have a sweet conversation about our marriage relationship and our relationship with God.

As I thought about this encounter, I recalled the scripture found in **Matthew 7:24-27 (NLT)**. *"Anyone who listens to my teaching and follows it is wise, like a person who builds a house on solid rock. Though the rain comes in torrents and the floodwaters rise and the winds beat against that house, it won't collapse because it is built on bedrock. But anyone who hears my* *teaching and doesn't obey it is foolish, like a person who builds a house on sand. When the rains and floods come and the winds beat against that house, it will collapse with a mighty crash."*

In our 50 years of marriage we have experienced those floodwaters and beating winds, but because the foundation of our relationship is based upon loving God, trusting God and obeying God, we have experienced the blessings God promises.

Many things have changed over the past 50 years. Our telephones were connected with wires and had rotary dials. We had to get up to change the channel on our black and white TV. We used typewriters and erasable bond paper so we could erase our mistakes. A dish was something you put your food on, not on your roof. Belts were used to hold up your pants, not to use in a car, and the front seat of a car was a bench that usually held three people. We brought our babies home in our arms, not in a car seat. Our meals were cooked in ovens and range tops, not in microwaves. We looked at the moon but had no idea someone would actually set foot upon it. We wrote letters on paper and sent them in the mail and text was something that a book had on its pages. A mouse was something that you didn't want in your house. You had to start your car with a key in the ignition. Paper maps were an essential aid while traveling. If you had a hole in your jeans you sewed a patch on it. An apple was a tasty fruit, not a computer. And I am sure some who reads this could add to the list.

But in the last 50 years and from the beginning of creation, one thing has not changed. God is the solid Rock. God is strong, He is our provider, He is our protection, He is unchanging, His Word is truth, and His love endures forever. Love God. Trust God. Obey

God. On this foundation, though things change, and life brings changes, God remains our solid rock where we will not be shaken.

Let all that I am wait quietly before God, for my hope is in him. He alone is my rock and my salvation, my fortress where I will not be shaken. My victory and honor come from God alone. He is my refuge, a rock where no enemy can reach me.
Psalm 62:5-7 (NLT)

"The LORD lives! Praise to my Rock! May God, the Rock of my salvation, be exalted!
2 Samuel 22:47 (NLT)

~ Illuminating Life Lessons ~

~ Illuminating Life Lessons ~

Not "Why?" but "What?"

**Life Lesson: Pain is unavoidable.
Misery is optional.**

Let's face it. We have an enemy who is very busy. He attacks in many different ways. He does not rest. Throughout the scriptures we read accounts of Satan's schemes to bring us down. When we are faced with challenges, all too often we ask the question, "Why?" Often that question is followed by a simple two letter word – "me." "Why me?" we ask. And in doing so, the enemy has accomplished his first and most effective blow. He has caused us to focus inward. He has directed our attention to our circumstance and more often than not, our inability to deal with the difficulty. This can lead to a downward spiral that ends in depression, bitterness and despair – right where the enemy wants us.

Because I have experienced this in my own life, I can write about it with authority. That pit of despair, filled with questions, doubts and fears is a lonely place to be. Too often I was unable or unwilling to share my pain, so I "lived with it." It wasn't a good companion. My mind was always occupied with that question. "Why?" Over and over the declaration, "I don't understand!" Thoughts turned to tears. Fears resulted in despair. Hope seemed lost.

Only recently has the burden been lifted to such an extent that I am amazed. It was an ordinary day, not unlike the others when I was plagued with questions. In His unique way, God had exposed me to two new thoughts. Yield. Believe.

These thoughts filled my mind with new possibilities. Hope. Joy. Peace.

I had reached a crossroads and had to choose which path I would take. One led to a sad, confusing place. That was not a place where I wanted to dwell. That was not a place where God would take me. That place of accusation, guilt and fear is where the enemy would take me.

God used these thoughts to put a new question in my mind. "What?" What is it that God wants to teach me? What work is God doing in this situation? This new question led me down a different path. Though I cannot see it, or understand it, I know, because of His character, that God is working out things for good. Perhaps that good is for me, or perhaps it is not about me at all. Whatever it might be, I must trust God. I must yield the situation to God. This "yielding" is not a one-time event, for the enemy is relentless in his efforts to bring me back into the pit.

Now when I sense the doubts arising, it becomes exciting to ask, "What, Lord? What are you teaching me?" I am filled with hope,

~ Illuminating Life Lessons ~

security and peace. I experience the stretching of my faith as I watch to see how God is working in this situation. I know that in time, His work will become clear and I will see His plan and purpose. And I believe – I know – because it is God at work, I will experience victory. That is the place God wants to take me.

So, I have made a choice. Even in the midst of pain, I choose to praise God. I choose to focus on His goodness, His faithfulness, His unfailing love. Yes, I choose to praise God. He is victorious. He defeats the enemy. I choose to claim His victory. Today I am filled with anticipation…with hope. Today I choose to ask not "Why?" but "What?" And I wait – expectantly.

Let me hear of your unfailing love each morning, for I am trusting you. Show me where to walk, for I give myself to you. Rescue me from my enemies, LORD; I run to you to hide me. Teach me to do your will, for you are my God. May your gracious Spirit lead me forward on a firm footing.
Psalm 143:8-10 (NLT)

~ Illuminating Life Lessons ~

According to your Faith

Life Lesson: God is ready and able to respond when I put my faith in Him.

In **Hebrews 11:1 (NLT)** we read, *"Faith shows the reality of what we hope for; it is the evidence of things we cannot see."* While traveling in New England off the coast of Cape Cod, I saw a ship far in the distance of a great expanse of just water and sky. I was in the same waters that the Pilgrims traveled when they first came to start a new life in America. With high hopes that they were headed to a new and better life, men and women journeyed to a place they had never seen. What tremendous faith it must have taken to endure the hardships they faced.

Even though we are blessed with provision, we too face hardships much like those recorded in the Bible. In the New Testament we find accounts where Jesus commends the faith of those who come to Him, trusting that He is able to do what would seem impossible. The Roman officer had faith that Jesus could heal his servant by simply speaking the word. The friends of a paralyzed man were so confident in Jesus' power that they lowered him on a mat through the roof. Jesus, seeing their faith, forgave the man of his sin and healed him, commanding, "Stand up, pick up your mat, and go home!" When the leader of a synagogue came to Jesus and declared by faith that even though his daughter had died, "You can bring her back to life again if you just come and lay your hand on her," Jesus faced the crowd that laughed at Him and as He took her hand, she stood up – alive.

While on His way to the official's home, a woman demonstrated her faith by simply touching Jesus' robe. Jesus said to her, "Daughter, be encouraged! Your faith has made you well." There are accounts of Jesus healing the blind, delivering a Gentile woman's daughter from a demon, healing those with leprosy, and filling a boat full of fish where there had been none. In each instance, Jesus responded to those who came to Him with faith, believing that He was able to meet their need by doing things that seemed impossible. The key in each instance is spoken by Jesus in **Matthew 9:28-30a (ESV)** *"When he entered the house, the blind men came to him, and Jesus said to them, "Do you believe that I am able to do this?" They said to him, "Yes, Lord." Then he touched their eyes, saying, "According to your faith be it done to you." And their eyes were opened."*

The records that reveal the tremendous hardship of those who traveled in the Mayflower paint a picture of pain, and despair, yet by faith they held on to the hope of what they could not yet see. Often, we find ourselves unable to see resolution when faced with the pain of challenges and difficulties. Just as those who encountered Jesus face to face, we must trust God. We must come to Him with unwavering faith believing that at all times and in every way, God is ready and able to meet our needs. **Isaiah 65:24 (NLT) tells us,** *"I will answer them before they even* *call to me. While they are still talking about their needs, I will go ahead and answer their prayers!"* Through these difficult times, God is working out something good in our life as well as in those we bring to Him in prayer.

Jesus gives us this invitation, *"Come to me, all of you who are weary and carry heavy burdens, and I will give you rest."* Matthew 11:28 (NLT) It is the goal of Satan to create chaos, stealing our peace. Let us declare our faith in the faithfulness of God and trust that at all times and in every way, God is ready and able.

And it is impossible to please God without faith. Anyone who wants to come to him must believe that God exists and that he rewards those who sincerely seek him. Hebrews 11:6 (NLT)

God is our refuge and strength, always ready to help in times of trouble. Psalm 46:1 (NLT)

Now all glory to God, who is able, through his mighty power at work within us, to accomplish infinitely more than we might ask or think. Ephesians 3:20 (NLT)

~ Illuminating Life Lessons ~

~ Illuminating Life Lessons ~

Declarations

Life Lesson: This I declare about the LORD: He alone is my refuge, my place of safety; he is my God, and I trust him. Psalms 91:2 (NLT)

On July 4, 1776, the Declaration of Independence was adopted by the Second Continental Congress. History tells us that the document had been passed on July 2 with no opposing vote cast. The purpose of the document was to formally explain why the thirteen American colonies were justified in separating from Great Britain. In it were listed the grievances against King George III as well as a statement that has been called "one of the best-known sentences in the English language." This passage came to represent a moral standard to which the United States should strive.

> "We hold these truths to be self-evident, that all men are created equal, that they are endowed by their Creator with certain unalienable Rights, that among these are Life, Liberty and the pursuit of Happiness."

With this document, our country's founders sought freedom from tyranny. Yet it became clear that "freedom is not free" as this document precipitated the Revolutionary War. Many laid down their lives to purchase the freedom we enjoy as Americans.

Still, as individuals we often face tyranny of another kind. Just as King George III sought to control and destroy this new nation, our enemy Satan seeks to *"steal and kill and destroy"* **John 10:10.** The freedom that God intended was stolen as a result of deception by the enemy. But we find in **1 Timothy 2:5-6 (NLT),** *"There is one God and one Mediator who can reconcile God and humanity—the man Christ Jesus. He gave his life to purchase freedom for everyone."*

Thus, we can make these declarations:

I am free from failure for *"I can do everything through Christ, who gives me strength."* Philippians 4:13

I am free from want for *"my God shall supply all my need according to His riches in Christ Jesus."* Philippians 4:19

I am free from fear for *"God has not given us a spirit of fear and timidity, but of power, love, and self-discipline."* 2 Timothy 1:7

I am free from doubt for *"When doubts filled my mind, your comfort gave me renewed hope and cheer."* Psalm 94:19

I am free from weakness for *"The Lord gives his people strength. The Lord blesses them with peace."* Psalm 29:11

~ Illuminating Life Lessons ~

I am free from the power of Satan for *"greater is He that is in me than he that is in the world."* 1 John 4:4

I am free from defeat for *"You are my hiding place; you protect me from trouble. You surround me with songs of victory."* Psalm 32:7

I am free from sin for *"the blood of Jesus, his Son, cleanses us from all sin."* 1 John 1:7

I am free from worry for I can *"Give all my worries and cares to God, for he cares about me."* 1 Peter 5:7

I am free from bondage for *"the Lord is the Spirit, and wherever the Spirit of the Lord is, there is freedom."* 2 Corinthians 3:17

I am free from strife for *"You will keep in perfect peace all who trust in You – all whose thoughts are fixed on You."* Isaiah 26:3

I am free from condemnation for *"now there is no condemnation for those who belong to Christ Jesus."* Romans 8:1

Just as our forefathers sought equality and rights for all in their declaration, God declared **"an end to sin's control over us by giving his Son as a sacrifice for our sins,"** Romans 8:3b.(NLT)

"Sin is no longer your master, for you no longer live under the requirements of the law. Instead, you live under the freedom of God's grace." Romans 6:14 (NLT)

As we celebrate Independence Day, let us celebrate our freedom purchased by the blood of Jesus Christ.

For you have been called to live in freedom, my brothers and sisters. But don't use your freedom to satisfy your sinful nature. Instead, use your freedom to serve one another in love.
Galatians 5:13 (NLT)

God Protects

Life Lesson: As we keep focused on God, obey, trust and love Him, God protects.

God's promise of protection is evident throughout the scriptures. In Genesis He promises to protect Abraham, in Exodus God sends an angel to guide and protect His people as they make their long journey to the promised land. We read how He protected Noah, Joseph, Daniel, the three in the furnace, David, even Job and countless others with His power and His deliverance. It's not as though these people were spared from difficulties. On the contrary, they faced difficulties that often seemed insurmountable. Yet God delivered them, demonstrating His power, His faithfulness, His love and protection.

In **Psalm 91 (NASB)** we find God's promise of protection. However, the promises found here are conditional. In verse 1 we read, *"He who dwells in the shelter of the Most High will abide in the shadow of the Almighty."* To dwell means to live in; to be settled; to stay; to keep the attention directed upon.

Verse 2 continues, *"I will say to the L*ORD*, "My refuge and my fortress, My God, in whom I trust!"* In verse 14a we read, *"Because he has loved Me, therefore I will deliver him."* So, we see that God's promises of protection are in place when we keep our attention directed upon Him, and when we trust God and love Him.

In verse 11 God gives this promise, **"For He will give His angels charge concerning you."** Angels are mentioned often in God's Word. They are given as an assurance of God's presence and watch care. In **Exodus 23:20 (NLT)** God gives His people this assurance as they escape from Egypt, *"See, I am sending an angel before you to protect you on your journey and lead you safely to the place I have prepared for you."*

Often in the scriptures, God is referred to as "The Lord of Heaven's Armies." In **Matthew 26:53 (NLT)** Jesus speaks of this heavenly army saying, *"Don't you realize that I could ask my Father for thousands of angels to protect us, and he would send them instantly?"*

Recently God's protection was demonstrated in an unmistakable manner. The granddaughter of my friend was traveling on a busy highway where the traffic often slows down and many times comes to a complete stop. As she approached the slower traffic, she could see that the cars were stopped. As she slowed and began to stop, she glanced in her rear-view mirror. She saw her two baby daughters safely sitting in their car seats and then saw a car approaching at a high speed. Fearing that she would be rear-ended she braced for the worst, but the car swerved, fishtailing as it passed, only sideswiping her car. What could have been a serious crash was only damage to the side of the car. All inside were safe with no injury. She said the babies didn't even cry.

When the accident account was relayed, someone said, "I'm glad that driver had enough sense to avoid rear-ending the car." I believe that The Lord of Heaven's Armies directed His angels to prevent the serious crash and delivered this young mother and her two babies from harm. Yes, there was trouble, but because this young mother loves and trusts God and has a grandmother who prays for her, she was protected and delivered from harm. In **Proverbs 2:8 (NLT)** we read, *"He guards the paths of the just and protects those who are faithful to him."* I am sure that there are many times when we face unknown danger, but as we keep focused on God, obey Him, trust Him and love Him, God protects.

God's way is perfect. All the LORD's promises prove true. He is a shield for all who look to him for protection.
2 **Samuel 22:31 (NLT)**

I AM - Willing

Life Lesson: In a healthy love relationship, there must be mutual sacrifice.

There are times when reading the Bible, I find a passage that causes me to pause, to meditate, to dig deep into its meaning. Recently I explored one of those passages. *"For God in all his fullness was pleased to live in Christ, and through him God reconciled everything to himself. He made peace with everything in heaven and on earth by means of Christ's blood on the cross."* Colossians 1:19-21 (NLT)

After looking up definitions of words and doing some research, this passage spoke to me in this way, **For God in all his fullness** (all that God is – every attribute – the sum total of His deity, His righteousness, power and love) **was pleased** (willing and glad; happy; satisfied) **to live in Christ,** (take on human flesh, face temptation, physically suffer) **and through him God reconciled** (restored a relationship; made peace; settled our differences) **everything to himself. He made peace with everything** (all that exists) **in heaven and on earth by means of Christ's blood on the**

cross. (The expression of God's justice and grace, reminding us of the serious nature and consequences of sin.)

This verse sums up the willingness of God to restore a relationship with mankind. In his book, *The Reason for God*, Tim Keller explains that in a healthy love relationship there must be mutual sacrifice. The parties must say, "I will adjust to you. I will change for you. I will serve you." In the most radical way, God has adjusted to us. He willingly became flesh and willingly fulfilled the justice required so that sin could no longer separate us from a relationship with Him.

How can it be that almighty God, the Great I AM is willing to serve me? Once again, I started digging. While in the presence of God at the burning bush, Moses asked, "When they ask me, 'What is His name?' What shall I say to them?" God responded, "I AM who I AM." There are many explanations, some from scholars, some from a biblical perspective, some from the dictionary. The name for God found in the King James version of the Bible is the four-letter name YHWH, a shortened version of YAHWEY. The Hebrew meaning is "the Self-existent," "He who becometh," or "the becoming one." One biblical definition of **I AM** is **"I will be who I will be."**

This open-ended response from God revealed to Moses a promise that He would become whatever they would need Him to become. What a promise! The unchanging God of Moses responds to us in the same way. He tells us, "For all that you lack and are not – I AM." This reveals that not only is God the all-sufficient One, He is willing to become what we need Him to be. God knew we needed a Savior.

~ Illuminating Life Lessons ~

In the beginning the Word already existed. The Word was with God, and the Word was God. So, the Word became human and made his home among us. He was full of unfailing love and faithfulness. And we have seen his glory, the glory of the Father's one and only Son. He existed in the beginning with God. John 1:1-2, 14 (NLT)

For God's will was for us to be made holy by the sacrifice of the body of Jesus Christ, once for all time Hebrews 10:10 (NLT)

When we were utterly helpless, Christ came at just the right time and died for us sinners. Now, most people would not be willing to die for an upright person, though someone might perhaps be willing to die for a person who is especially good. But God showed his great love for us by sending Christ to die for us while we were still sinners. Romans 5:6-8 (NLT)

God wants to show us what He can accomplish through us if we declare those same words, "I am – available, willing, trusting." Our mutual sacrifice is to give up our freedom in order to find freedom in Him. The resulting love relationship is possible only because the great **I AM is willing.**

~ Illuminating Life Lessons ~

God is Forgiving

Life Lesson: The sacrifice of Jesus' blood on the cross pays the penalty for my sin, frees me from guilt and restores my relationship with God.

When my granddaughter was younger, she was at my home and had done something that she knew was wrong. She was upset. I felt that I needed to take her aside and talk with her. As I sat with her, she was tearful and in agony, bearing the heavy weight of guilt. Hoping I could encourage her to ask for forgiveness, I told her to go to the person and say, "I'm sorry." Now she was sobbing, and she cried out, "I can't say I'm sorry! I can't! It's too hard!"

Have you ever been there? I have. It seems that there are times when it is easier to feel guilty than to ask forgiveness. The importance of acknowledging our sin, confessing it to God and repenting (turning away from sin) is essential. We read in *Isaiah 59:2 (NLT)* *"It's your sins that have cut you off from God. Because of your sins, he has turned away and will not listen anymore."* God promises in *1 John 1:9 (NLT)* *"But if we confess*

our sins to him, he is faithful and just to forgive us our sins and to cleanse us from all wickedness." All He asks is that we confess our sin – that we agree with what God already knows.

Not only does God forgive our sin, He chooses to forget our sin. We receive this assurance from God's Word in ***Isaiah 43:25 (NIV) "I, even I, am he who blots out your transgressions, for my own sake, and remembers your sins no more".*** God forgives – for His own sake. Why? Because He has paid the penalty for our sin. Because He desires a relationship with us.

Recently I saw a post on Facebook that read, "I forgive you. Forget you. The end." These were the closing lyrics of a song entitled *Dear Agony*. As I thought about those words, I realized two things. Humanly, words of forgiveness may end a relationship. Although the words are spoken, seeds of bitterness may still find fertile soil leaving no desire to continue a relationship, only leaving emptiness and pain.

But with God, forgiveness is not the end, but the beginning of a relationship. The sin, not the person is forgotten. Justice has been served by the One who forgives through the blood of Jesus Christ. No more shame, blame or guilt. Unlike those under the law who were required to follow strict rules as they offered sacrifices to cover their sin, we live under grace, that undeserved favor, which allows us to confess and repent of our sins and receive forgiveness. As we turn away from our sin, the result is healing and an overwhelming sense of love and gratitude to the One who forgives. No longer do we avoid being in God's presence. No longer do we hear the whispers of the enemy that we are unforgiveable.

Now we are filled with peace and assurance that is described in **Psalm 32:4-6 (NLT)** *"Day and night your hand of discipline was heavy on me. My strength evaporated like water in the summer heat. Finally, I confessed all my sins to you and stopped trying to hide my guilt. I said to myself, 'I will confess my rebellion to the LORD.' And you forgave me! All my guilt is gone."*

The blood of Jesus is sufficient to wash our soul clean. God has pardoned us, giving us freedom from the debt we owe because of our sin. We must only be obedient to confess our sin to Him and receive the forgiveness that He freely offers. When forgiven, we must choose to take off the cloak of guilt that the enemy would have us wear and rejoice in the newness of life that we receive. *"I am overwhelmed with joy in the LORD my God! For he has dressed me with the clothing of salvation and draped me in a robe of righteousness."* Isaiah 61:10a (NLT)

Just as we have been forgiven, may forgiveness become the beginning, the restoration of relationships and may we offer to others the gift of grace that has been given to us.

LORD, if you kept a record of our sins, who, O Lord, could ever survive? But you offer forgiveness that we might learn to fear you. Psalm 130:3-4 (NLT)

~ Illuminating Life Lessons ~

Forgiveness

Life Lesson: I cannot love until I forgive.

I have observed that relationships can be broken due to a lack of forgiveness. As humans, we all have certain priorities that we may consider more important than those of another. These differences can lead to feelings of offense and seem unforgivable. We must determine which is more important, the feelings of being offended or the relationship. We must ask ourselves, "Can I forgive?"

I was reading the account of King David in **2 Samuel 12**, where his sin of taking the life of Uriah was exposed. I then turned to **Psalm 51** which is described as David's prayer for pardon. In this Psalm David vividly expresses the heaviness of sin. David is desperately seeking forgiveness. He cries out, *"Have mercy on me, O God, because of your unfailing love." "Against you, and you alone, have I sinned. I have done what is evil in your sight." "Do not banish me from your presence, and don't take your Holy Spirit from me."* David appears to fear that because of his sin, God would no longer love him. As I was thinking about forgiveness, this thought came to my mind. "You can't love until you forgive."

After Adam and Eve brought sin into the world through their disobedience, the only way the relationship that they enjoyed with God could be restored was through forgiveness. In **Hebrews 10:1-7 (NLT)** we read, *"The old system under the law of Moses was only a shadow, a dim preview of the good things to come, not the good things themselves. The sacrifices under that system were repeated again and again, year after year, but they were never able to provide perfect cleansing for those who came to worship. If they could have provided perfect cleansing, the sacrifices would have stopped, for the worshipers would have been purified once for all time, and their feelings of guilt would have disappeared. But instead, those sacrifices actually reminded them of their sins year after year. For it is not possible for the blood of bulls and goats to take away sins."*

"That is why, when Christ came into the world, he said to God, "You did not want animal sacrifices or sin offerings. But you have given me a body to offer. You were not pleased with burnt offerings or other offerings for sin. Then I said, 'Look, I have come to do your will, O God—as is written about me in the Scriptures.'"

This led me to consider my relationship with God. Before I could experience God's love, I had to acknowledge my sin and receive His forgiveness. It also helped me realize that before I can give love, I must forgive. And not only must I forgive, I must forgive as God forgives – *"And I will forgive their wickedness, and I will never again remember their sins."* **Hebrews 10:12 (NLT)** I cannot say, "I forgive," but keep the offense on a back shelf in my mind. I must let it go. If I hold unforgiveness in my heart, it blocks God's love from flowing through me. That thought, "You can't love until you forgive," rings true.

Consider the great cost of God's forgiveness for mankind. The desire of God from the beginning was to have a loving relationship with mankind. After sin entered the world, the only way He could restore the broken relationship was to forgive. In order to do that He had to become a limited human being, live a simple life, overcome the temptations of Satan, physically and emotionally suffer, and obediently crawl upon a cross and die. When Jesus cried out, *"My God, my God, why have you forsaken me?"* he carried the sin of all mankind. Though he cried out for God's love, it could not be found. Yet through this act of sacrifice, God was able to offer forgiveness and restore the love relationship He intended from the beginning of creation.

Mother Theresa once said, *"If we really want to love, we must learn how to forgive."* Until we can forgive, we cannot love completely. Just as it cost God a great sacrifice, we, too, must be willing to sacrifice in order to experience the freedom to love. God's love for us started with forgiveness. May we follow His example.

Love prospers when a fault is forgiven, but dwelling on it separates close friends. Proverbs 17:9 (NLT)

~ Illuminating Life Lessons ~

~ Illuminating Life Lessons ~

God Gives Freedom

Life Lesson: Forgiveness sets me free.

As I watched a television show recently, one of the scenes stirred my thoughts. A man who had committed a terrible crime was behind bars in prison and the person standing outside the bars was the victim. This victim's life would never be the same and it was clear that his heart was full of hate. Glad that the criminal was behind bars, he taunted him as he stood outside the prison cell. Then, in a calm voice, the prisoner said to the victim, "You will always be my prisoner."

There is a prison that we willingly enter. It is the prison of unforgiveness. This prison is a place of unrest, turmoil, bitterness and despair. When we are unwilling to forgive, Satan declares, "You will always be my prisoner." Held hostage by an unwillingness to forgive those who sin against us, we face being subject to sin ourselves. Greg Laurie, pastor of Harvest Church, put it this way. *"Unforgiveness is choosing to love hate. It produces bitterness, anger, rage, anxiety, and depression. Simply put, it is sin. Instead, we must forgive."*

Jesus taught His disciples about forgiveness. When teaching them about prayer, He included in the Lord's prayer, *"...and forgive us our sins, as we have forgiven those who sin against us."* He continues in **Matthew 6:14-15 (NLT)** *"If you forgive those who sin against you, your heavenly Father will forgive you. But if you refuse to forgive others, your Father will not forgive your sins."* Although our forgiveness is based upon the shed blood of Jesus Christ, we must confess the sin of unforgiveness so that we can be forgiven. *But if we confess our sins to him, he is faithful and just to forgive us our sins and to cleanse us from all wickedness.* **1 John 1:9 (NLT)**

Very clearly Jesus tells us, to be forgiven, we must forgive. Until we do, we will find ourselves in that dreaded place, the prison of unforgiveness. The bars of this prison separate us from human relationships and from a peaceful relationship with God.

Although the chains of unforgiveness confine us, there is hope for freedom. It starts with repentance. You may ask, "Why must I repent? I am not the one who sinned." We read in **Romans 2:2 (NLT)** *"Don't copy the behavior and customs of this world, but let God transform you into a new person by changing the way you think."* It is so easy to think vengeful thoughts when we are unwilling to forgive, but the key that unlocks the door of the prison of unforgiveness requires a choice. *"That means you must not give sin a vote in the way you conduct your lives. Don't give it the time of day. Don't even run little errands that are connected with that old way of life. Throw yourselves wholeheartedly and full-time—remember, you've been raised from the dead! —into God's way of doing things. Sin can't tell you how to live. After all, you're not living under that old* *tyranny any longer. You're living in the freedom of God."* **Romans 6:12-14 (MSG)** And in **Exodus 34:6-7** we read that God is compassionate and gracious, slow to anger, abounding in lovingkindness and truth, and forgiving of iniquity, transgressions and sin. That is our God. He forgives.

We must offer to others what God has offered us. Forgiveness. Because of His love and His mercy, God did not dwell on our sin, but set in place a plan for our forgiveness. Through the blood of Jesus Christ, we are no longer prisoners of sin. He has set us free. When we forgive, God gives freedom, setting us free from the prison of unforgiveness.

So, we praise God for the glorious grace he has poured out on us who belong to his dear Son. He is so rich in kindness and grace that he purchased our freedom with the blood of his Son and forgave our sins. Ephesians 1:6-7(NLT)

~ Illuminating Life Lessons ~

~ Illuminating Life Lessons ~

Pulling Weeds

Life Lesson: Even when we go about our daily tasks like pulling weeds, God has something He wants to teach us.

God is continually teaching me through His creation. I greatly enjoy planting a small garden in the spring and in the fall. One year I neglected my garden after the early summer harvest and weeds started to grow. Life brought some challenges that kept me from taking care of the garden, and by fall planting time, the entire plot was covered in a grass type weed that was over 12 inches tall. My dear husband cleared out the weeds and I planted my garden, but the harvest was much less than I had hoped.

The next spring, I pulled the visible weeds but once again my garden did not produce as it had before. I was determined to get rid of every weed before the next planting season, so I got a shovel and dug deep to make sure the roots were gone. I applied new garden soil and waited for the hot summer to pass. Each day I checked to see that no weeds were growing, and the soil appeared free of any growth. Because of the weather conditions my planting was delayed but it appeared that the weeds were gone once and for all.

About a week after planting, the little seedlings started to pop out of the soil. Each day when I first got up, I looked out the window to see how they had grown. On one morning I noticed that something had changed and when I looked closer, I could see that my garden was covered in tiny blades of the weed I thought I had purged. Not wanting it to take over again, I started pulling up the tiny plants and as I did, I noticed that the roots seemed to be attached to an underlying network that lay like a blanket under the entire garden. Because I had neglected the garden and let the weeds grow tall, I now had a major problem. Even though the garden was growing nicely, each day I had to pull the tiny weeds that would take over if I were to ignore them.

Weeds. Some are big and some are tiny - barely noticeable - but regardless of their size or type, they are all the same. They are weeds. God showed me that this is a picture of sin. Some things we consider to be big sins, others small sins, but in God's eyes, they are all the same. They are sin.

Because of the fall of man, we all have an underlying sin nature, and just like that network of roots in my garden, sin will show itself if we are not vigilant. Our attitudes of pride, unforgiveness, judgements, or resentment can stunt our spiritual growth and cause our relationship with God to weaken. Until we acknowledge our sin, confess, repent and renounce our sin, it can grow in harmful ways.

Some will say, "But I am just human," using this as an excuse for allowing sin to remain in their lives. We must not minimize the power of the Holy Spirit. **In 2 Peter 1:3(NLT)** we read, *"By his divine power, God has given us everything we need for living a godly life. We have received all of this by coming to know him, the one who called us to himself by means of his marvelous glory and excellence."* God's Word also tells us that a wonderful thing happens when we yield to the Holy Spirit. *"**But the Holy Spirit produces this kind of fruit in our lives: love, joy, peace, patience, kindness, goodness, faithfulness, gentleness, and self-control.**"* Galatians 5:22-23a (NLT) Notice that God's Word does not say that we must work hard to achieve the fruit, rather it says that the Holy Spirit produces the fruit. A harvest of goodness is produced within us. What we must do is yield our thoughts, words and deeds to the power of the Holy Spirit.

What does that look like? **John 14:26 (NLT)** Tells us, *"But when the Father sends the Advocate as my representative—that is, the Holy Spirit—he will teach you everything and will remind you of everything I have told you."* Here we see that we must listen to what God teaches us, through His Word as well as when He "speaks" to our heart. Then we must choose to live by the power of the Holy Spirit as stated in **Galatians 5:16 (NLT)** *"So I say, let the Holy Spirit guide your lives. Then you won't be doing what your sinful nature craves."*

I have not discovered a remedy for the weeds in my garden, but every day I search for the tiny weeds and pull them up. As I hear the crunch of the roots breaking away from that network that still remains, I am reminded to ask the Holy Spirit to examine my heart. When sin is revealed I confess it and receive forgiveness. Then I make a choice to repent - to turn in the opposite direction. Considering the consequences of sin, I also must renounce it - abandon it. If or when it resurfaces, I must say, "No more." God taught me through my garden to be on the alert and not let sin gain a foothold in my life. When I listen, He teaches me - even while I am pulling weeds.

Search me, O God, and know my heart; test me and know my anxious thoughts. Point out anything in me that offends you and lead me along the path of everlasting life.
Psalm 139:23-24 (NLT)

~ Illuminating Life Lessons ~

Choices

Life Lesson: My choices shape my life as well as the lives of others.

Recently I was listening to the news and the person being interviewed had, in the past, gone through a terrifying period in her life. Now she is happily married with a family of her own, helping others who have experienced similar trauma. The interviewer asked her how she was able recover and overcome the past. She made a simple statement that to me was profound and began to stir several thoughts in my mind that I want to share. The statement was simply, "It is our choices that make us who we are."

Choices. Each day, moment by moment we are making choices. Often, we have daily routines and are unaware that we are acting due to a choice that has been made. What time we get up. When we brush our teeth. What we have for breakfast, lunch or dinner. What tasks we engage in or what job we go to. How we react to those we encounter. How many cups of coffee or tea we drink.

How we spend our leisure time. What time we go to bed. And that's just our daily routine choices.

We make life choices that help shape us as individuals. What education path we take. Do we choose to marry? If so, what type of person do we share our life with, or do we choose to end that relationship? What kind of friends we have. How we take care of our body – food choices, exercise, medications. Our hobbies or activities such as clubs or church or shopping. I could go on and on. Some choices are easy, others are difficult. Some are positive choices, others we regret. For a moment, stop and consider how many choices we must make in a day, a week, a month, a year or in a lifetime. How have these choices shaped your life?

There are some situations in our life where we have no choice. Perhaps it is our parents, our children or as the person who was interviewed, a life situation that is forced upon us. Yet still, we can choose how we react to the situation. Those choices will also affect "who we are."

So, who are we? God's Word helps us answer that question. In **Isaiah 43:7 (NLT)** we read, *"Bring all who claim me as their God, for I have made them for my glory. It was I who created them.'"* We were created by God to bring glory to God. Yet, even in this verse we see a choice. Do we choose to acknowledge and worship God? After bringing the Israelites to the Promised Land, in a farewell address Joshua reviews Israel's history recalling all the ways that God has preserved His people. He challenges the people to make a choice. He says, *"But if you refuse to serve the Lord, then choose today whom you will serve. Would you prefer the gods your ancestors served beyond the Euphrates? Or will it be the gods of the Amorites in whose land you now live? But as* *for me and my family, we will serve the LORD."* Joshua 24:15 (NLT)

In 1979, after becoming a Christian, Bob Dylan wrote a song about finding meaning in life through serving God. The lyrical message was:

> "You're gonna have to serve somebody.
> You're gonna have to serve somebody.
> Well, it may be the devil, or it may be the Lord,
> but you're gonna have to serve somebody."

How would our choices differ if we considered this as our every day alternative?

If we were created to bring glory to God, how do we do that? Jesus was asked this question and His answer is found in **Matthew 22:37-40 (NLT).** *Jesus replied, "'You must love the LORD your God with all your heart, all your soul, and all your mind.' This is the first and greatest commandment. A second is equally important: 'Love your neighbor as yourself.' The entire law and all the demands of the prophets are based on these two commandments."* How we bring glory to God? The answer is LOVE. Love God. Love others.

In **1 Corinthians 13:4-7 (NLT)** we discover how to make choices to love others.

> I choose to be patient and kind.
> I choose not to be jealous or boastful or proud or rude.
> I choose not to demand my own way.
> I choose not to be irritable.

I choose not to keep a record of being wronged.
I choose to rejoice when truth wins out, not to rejoice about injustice.
I choose to never give up.
I choose never to lose faith.
I choose to always be hopeful.
I choose to love unconditionally through every circumstance.

When God created us, He gave us free will. He allows us to make choices. That includes the choice to love and serve Him. **Deuteronomy 7:9 (NLT)** helps us understand why choosing to love God is a good choice. *"Understand, therefore, that the LORD your God is indeed God. He is the faithful God who keeps his covenant for a thousand generations and lavishes his unfailing love on those who love him and obey his commands."* God demonstrates His love for us in countless ways. We see Him in creation. Through Him we have hope, joy and peace. He offers the gift of forgiveness and salvation. His love endures forever.

Choices. Ultimately our choices make us who we are. Who will you choose to be today?

> **My words are plain to anyone with understanding,**
> **clear to those with knowledge.**
> **Choose my instruction rather than silver,**
> **and knowledge rather than pure gold.**
> **For wisdom is far more valuable than rubies.**
> **Nothing you desire can compare with it.**
> **Proverbs 8:9-11(NLT)**

~ Illuminating Life Lessons ~

Side Effects

Life Lesson: People might forget what you've said, but they will always remember how you made them feel.

I am always amazed how God teaches us profound lessons through ordinary every-day things we experience. Let me be transparent with you today. Recently I took a new medication to alleviate pain I experienced as I tried to sleep. The medicine worked like a charm and I slept soundly and long without pain. I was thrilled because I was resting better than I had for many months. I continued taking the medication but noticed that my vision was becoming blurry and it was hard to focus. This was somewhat alarming to me. I thought to myself, "I've put off getting glasses for so long, but now it must be time to make an appointment with the eye doctor." I had recently gained a few extra pounds and noticed that my feet and ankles were a bit swollen with what seemed to be retained fluid. Once again, I thought it must just be my age, but it seemed unusually uncomfortable.

I couldn't explain why these things suddenly happened and decided to investigate the side effects of my new medication. There it was – blurred vision, fluid retention especially in the feet and ankles, weight gain. The side effects of the medication were exactly what I had experienced. I immediately stopped taking the medication and within one day, my vision was back to normal and the fluid in my feet was gone. I had even lost a couple of pounds almost overnight. Those side effects had snuck up on me so gradually I barely noticed them until they affected me adversely.

I was relieved and thankful, but as I thought of what I had experienced, I realized that God was teaching me through it all. I began to ask myself, "What are the side effects of my actions, my attitudes, my words, even the tone of my speech?" Shortly after I began to consider this, my daughter, respectfully but clearly asked me to examine the tone of my words. I was unaware that the tone of my words spoken to others at times fit the description found in **Psalm 52:2a (NLT)** *"Your tongue cuts like a sharp razor."* God was clearly speaking to me.

This led to a time of self-examination and prayer. I realized that the tone of my words was colored by my attitude toward those to whom I spoke. I had allowed unfulfilled expectations and unforgiveness to grow a root of bitterness in my spirit and it spilled out in my words. God allowed the circumstances in my life to converge into a life transforming moment. I had been unaware of how I had been hurting those I love. It was as though the side effects of my words had gradually increased until they had become toxic.

In **1 Peter 5:8(NLT)** we read, *"Stay alert! Watch out for your great enemy, the devil. He prowls around like a roaring lion,* *looking for someone to devour."* Think of it. A lion seeking its prey doesn't roar, it stealthily creeps up so that it isn't noticed until it is too late for the prey to escape. Then, after successfully capturing the prey, he roars in victory. All too often the side effects of our words and attitudes creep upon us and we don't realize it until the damage has been done, then Satan declares victory. People might forget what you've said, but they will always remember how you made them feel.

God gives us several warnings about not only our enemy, Satan, but our words, attitudes and actions. In the book of James and many other passages in God's Word we are warned about the power of the tongue. Our words have side effects and when spoken cannot be taken back. I once heard a preacher suggest that before I speak, I must ask myself, "Is it true? Is it kind? Is it confidential? Is it necessary?"

God's Word gives us instruction for each of these questions.
Is it true? Psalm 34:13 (NLT) Then keep your tongue from speaking evil and your lips from telling lies!
Is it kind? Proverbs 16:24 (NLT) Kind words are like honey— sweet to the soul and healthy for the body.
Is it confidential? Proverbs 11:13 (NLT) A gossip goes around telling secrets, but those who are trustworthy can keep a confidence.
Is it necessary? Psalm 141:3 (NLT) Take control of what I say, O LORD, and guard my lips.

As I follow this advice, I have come to realize that many of the things that come to mind need not be spoken. They are simply unnecessary. I realize that the side effects of my words can become life or death to those who hear them.

I found encouragement in **Ephesians 4:31-32 (NLT)** *"Get rid of all bitterness, rage, anger, harsh words, and slander, as well as all types of evil behavior. Instead, be kind to each other, tenderhearted, forgiving one another, just as God through Christ has forgiven you."* Just as medications have both good and bad side effects, so can our words. As He continues to teach me, I want my words to bring life, to build others up and to point them to God.

> **May the words of my mouth and the meditation of my heart be pleasing to you, O Lord, my rock and my redeemer.**
> **Psalm 19:14 (NLT)**

~ Illuminating Life Lessons ~

Grace

Life Lesson: God is the source of all grace. I am the distributer of His grace.

When my 93-year-old mother was carried by angels into the arms of Jesus, the grace of God was demonstrated to me and my family over and over in so many ways as we traveled through this difficult journey. Grace is sometimes referred to as unmerited favor. Although we do not deserve it and because we cannot earn it, God meets our every need at those times when we are empty – when we are lost – when we are in need of that which we cannot even express in words. God is faithful to pour out His love and grace in ways that can only be explained by the fact that He loves us with an eternal, unconditional, unfailing love. He uses those who are sensitive to His loving Holy Spirit to distribute that amazing grace.

When we experience the homegoing of a loved one, I am so thankful that through the grace of God we have hope. In **Romans 5:17 (NLT)** we read, *"For the sin of this one man, Adam, caused death to rule over many. But even greater is God's wonderful* *grace and his gift of righteousness, for all who receive it will live in triumph over sin and death through this one man, Jesus Christ."*

As I saw the life of my mother slowly slipping into eternity, I was filled with hope. Because of God's grace and His gift of salvation, my relationship with my mother had changed, but had not ended. The hope of eternal life in heaven with our loved ones who have received His gift of salvation through Jesus Christ is more than just a hope – it is truth. In **John 1:14 (NIV)** we read, *"The Word became flesh and made his dwelling among us. We have seen his glory, the glory of the one and only Son, who came from the Father, full of grace and truth."*

Paul stated in his letter to Timothy. *"The grace of our Lord was poured out on me abundantly, along with the faith and love that are in Christ Jesus."* **1 Timothy 1:14 (NIV).** I experienced this personally as the hands of caregivers gently helped my mother meet her physical needs. The power of prayer was poured out over my mother and our family filling our hearts with God's perfect peace. Neighbors provided food that was timely and abundant. Hugs were freely offered and gratefully received. As the family shared their last words at the final service, it was evident that God had blessed us all with a mother who was an instrument of God's grace, distributing it personally and specifically to each of us according to our need.

While God pours out His grace upon us, we can be distributers of His grace as He directs us to those who are in need, using our hands, our hearts and the resources He has provided to pour out His grace. When you see those who need a touch of God's grace, become a volunteer and don't hold back - distribute it abundantly and freely.

May our Lord Jesus Christ himself and God our Father, who loved us and by his grace gave us eternal encouragement and good hope, encourage your hearts and strengthen you in every good deed and word. 2 Thessalonians 2:15-17 (NIV)

~ Illuminating Life Lessons ~

God is Prodigal

Life Lesson: Many accounts found in the Bible have much deeper meaning than first appears. Dig deep into God's Word and find the treasures it holds.

Perhaps you reacted to this title as I first did. When I considered the meaning of the word "prodigal" I thought of a person who left the family and acted foolishly as in the parable Jesus taught in **Luke chapter 15**. Often, we refer to a prodigal child as one who leaves the family with no desire to return. When I looked for the definition of the word "prodigal" I found that I was totally wrong. I discovered that there are two definitions, both of which are revealed through this parable. First the word 'prodigal' is defined as "spending money or resources freely and recklessly; wastefully extravagant." The second definition is "having or giving something on a lavish scale; unsparing."

Now let's look deep into this parable and see why we can say that, yes, God is prodigal. My insights come from a book I recently read by Tim Keller, *The Prodigal God*. I had read this passage in the Bible many times and had always focused on the foolish younger son who seemed to squander his portion of what should have been a future inheritance. I confess that I sided with the older son who, in spite of his obedience to the family, appeared to be unfairly treated in favor of his foolish brother.

You see, the younger son requested his half of the inheritance he was entitled to receive upon his father's death. This cost the father half of his wealth. After receiving his inheritance, the son left the family and fulfilled the first definition stated above. His disrespect for his father and immoral reckless behavior led him on a path of destruction. With the inheritance squandered, he ended up dining with the pigs. Realizing that he had nothing left, he returned home, humble and willing to be treated as a servant. But instead of being turned away, he was joyfully welcomed home by his father. He was given new clothes, a big party and was reinstated as a rightful heir of what was left of the inheritance.

Obviously, that did not set well with the older son. After all, now his father's wealth was only half of what it had been. He refused to join the celebration and presented his case to the father. He felt that he had been treated unfairly. After all, he protested that he had been slaving for his father and never disobeyed. Shouldn't this earn him the favor of his father? Never had the father allowed him to have a big party with his friends. He realized that his half of the inheritance would now be shared with his brother. He was angry. I could see his point. How could the father behave in this manner? Then I realized that something within my heart had been revealed.

~ Illuminating Life Lessons ~

As Tim Keller explored the parable, he revealed that there were two kinds of people represented in the story – and they both were the same. By the end of the story, both at one time had been alienated from the father. The younger son had acknowledged his sinful ways and had returned to the father in humility. The older son at the end of the parable has not responded to the father's plea to have a change of heart and join in the celebration. The younger son had been foolish and sinful, and the older son had been judgmental and unforgiving. I saw myself in both sons. For many years I hoped my "good works" would earn favor with God. Later I realized my need for a Savior, confessed my sins and received forgiveness. Although my relationship with God remains unchanging, at times I display attitudes that can alienate me from fellowship with God.

This parable also teaches us about the father. I am sure that the father was heartbroken when his younger son left the family. It is revealed that he had been watching for his son to return, for when he returned, the father saw his son coming from a distance. When he saw his son coming, rather than reprimanding him, the father opened his arms and was filled with compassion and joy. As the son asked for forgiveness the father's love for his son was expressed unsparingly.

And that is a picture of our Heavenly father. The compassionate love and forgiveness God offers to us is given on a lavish scale. It cost Him dearly. He paid for it with blood as Jesus died on the cross. Now I understand that although the parable relates the story of two sons, both of whom need forgiveness, it is more about the father. It is also about me. I am eternally grateful that God responded to my plea for forgiveness and draped me in His robe of righteousness. Now I see even more clearly that because

He willingly, unsparingly gives His love and forgiveness, God is prodigal.

> I am overwhelmed with joy in the LORD my God! For he has dressed me with the clothing of salvation and draped me in a robe of righteousness. Isaiah 61:10a (NLT)

> See what great love the Father has lavished on us, that we should be called children of God! And that is what we are!
> 1 John 3:1a (NIV)

Don't Steal

Life Lesson: God reveals His glory when we trust in His provision.

Recently I attended a church where the pastor was teaching a series entitled The Relationship Principles behind the Ten Commandments. I had always thought of the Ten Commandments as moral laws by which we should guide our lives. Never had I considered that each commandment had an underlying principle that was meant to enhance our relationship with God. This message was based on the commandment found in **Exodus 20:15 (NLT)**, *"You must not steal."* I had always considered this to be a law that must be obeyed in order to avoid the consequences of punishment. I learned that God has much more for us to glean from His Word.

Before the Ten Commandments were revealed to the Israelites, conditions were worsening as they traveled. After about one month they had evidently consumed the food they brought with them and they complained that they were starving. In **Exodus 16:6b-7a (NLT)** Moses tells the people, *"By evening you will *realize it was the* L ORD *who brought you out of the land of Egypt. In the morning <u>you will see the glory of the</u>* L ORD, *because he has heard your complaints".* Then in **Exodus 16:11-12 (NLT)** we read, **"Then the L ORD said to Moses, "I have heard the Israelites' complaints. Now tell them, 'In the evening you will have meat to eat, and in the morning, you will have all the bread you want. Then you will know that I am the L ORD your God.'"** If I had been there in the middle of nowhere, I am sure I would have questioned where this provision would come from. No grain, no oil = no bread. But this was about more than just food. The relationship principle was trust. God was testing His people to see if they would trust Him. God wanted His people to know that He would be their provider and His glory (high renown, distinction, honor won by notable achievements) would be revealed.

To satisfy their hunger for meat He sent quail that evening, then each morning He provided manna, instructing the people to gather only enough for each day. On the sixth day in order to have provision for the Sabbath they were to gather a two-day supply. Those who did not follow the instructions and gathered more than they should revealed their lack of trust. They were surprised the next day to see the extra manna full of maggots.

So often, just like those who took extra manna, we show our lack of trust in God. **Philippians 4:19 (NIV)** states, **"And my God will meet all your needs according to the riches of his glory in Christ Jesus."** God's provision is boundless, yet at times we try to get ahead of His provision, taking things into our own hands. All too often, we put our trust in God only when we have exhausted our own resources. God wants us to enjoy a relationship of trust. As we consider Noah, Moses, Abraham, Daniel and many others from God's Word, we see that those who trusted God and followed Him in obedience enjoyed His provision.

This leads us back to the commandment, *"You must not steal."* When we become self-sufficient, taking matters into our own hands, not trusting God, all too often we find "maggots" invading our lives. Yes, matters may work out because of our efforts, and when they do, we enjoy a sense of achievement and pride. But when this happens, have we broken God's commandment?

"What are we stealing?" you might ask. We are stealing God's glory. Just as He tested the Israelites, He tests us and when we wait, trusting in God's provision, His glory is revealed. The very purpose for which man was created is declared in **Isaiah 43:7(NLT)**, *"Bring all who claim me as their God, for I have made them for my glory."* Experiencing the glory of God is life transforming, for it leads us to a place of trust. So, the principle behind the commandment, "You must not steal," reminds us that God is our provider. He desires for us to know Him, to enjoy a relationship of trust, to see His glory revealed and to give Him glory.

> Wealth and honor come from you alone, for you rule over everything. Power and might are in your hand, and at your discretion people are made great and given strength. O our God, we thank you and praise your glorious name!
> 1 Chronicles 29:12-13 (NLT)

~ Illuminating Life Lessons ~

~ Illuminating Life Lessons ~

Stress

Life Lesson: "Stress" is not a thing; it is how we choose to react to the unknown in our lives.

Several years ago, my mother had a minor stroke. Although I had to transport her to the grocery store, to doctor appointments and other errands, she was able to remain living in her home alone safely. In time her situation started to change dramatically. Because of changes in her behavior and reasoning ability my husband and I knew that, even though we were only a block away, she was no longer safe while home alone. The stress of trying to help her with daily needs weighed heavily upon us and we were asking ourselves, "What are we going to do?" Daily we worked through the possibilities but with limited resources we could not formulate a plan that would meet her needs as well as ours. The stress of the situation was growing each day.

Some time ago I read this statement. "Stress does not exist." You may be thinking as I did, "Really? I am stressed more often than I can count!" I began to question this statement. Is stress something I can touch? Can I see it or describe what it looks like?

Oh, yes, I see the effects of stress in a person, but what exactly is it? I began to realize that stress is something we conjure up and put upon ourselves. I saw how I had been so focused on trying to solve the situation for my mom that I had let it overtake my peace of mind.

Perhaps you have experienced stress in some way as I have. So how can we stop "stressing out?" The answer to "stress relief" is not a pill or a potion – it is trust. Where stress steals our peace, trust gives us peace. But all too often, yielding to stress is much easier than doing the work of trusting. Trusting requires yielding to the unknown. Letting go of worry about the future. God's Word reminds us in **Philippians 4:6-7 (NLT)** *"Don't worry about anything; instead, pray about everything. Tell God what you need, and thank him for all he has done. Then you will experience God's peace, which exceeds anything we can understand. His peace will guard your hearts and minds as you live in Christ Jesus."* When we focus on the One who holds our future, the One whose love endures forever, the One who is good, the One who is faithful, the One in whom we can confidently place our trust, we find ourselves in a place of peace – regardless of our circumstances.

God knew my mother's needs and He knew that we needed His help. One of the ladies in my Bible study group was sharing about similar needs for her mom. She shared some information that started a chain of events that God had planned before time began. As we prayed for His guidance it was evident that He was a step ahead of us throughout each day. He led us through a door which led to another door. It was evident that God had a specific plan for my mother. Within eleven days we had found a new home for my mother where she would be safe and cared for by lovely Christian people. Here she would get the extra personal care she needed.

Just a few days before she moved to her new home, we celebrated her 93rd birthday. It was a happy day. One that she would not remember. Through this season of life God reminded me in His Word, *"The Lord says, "I will rescue those who love me. I will protect those who trust in my name. When they call on me, I will answer; I will be with them in trouble. I will rescue and honor them."* Psalm 91:14-15 (NLT)

Life is filled with "unknowns." When stress starts to stir within you, don't let it steal your peace. Recognize that "stress" is not a thing, it is how we react to the unknown in our lives. And we have a choice. Choose to put on the burden of stress or choose to put your trust in God. When you choose to bring your cares and concerns to Him, trusting God to be your guide, and following His lead, you will experience peace.

You will keep in perfect peace all who trust in you, all whose thoughts are fixed on you! Isaiah 26:3 (NLT)

~ Illuminating Life Lessons ~

God is Peace

Life Lesson: Shift your focus from what you can do to what God can do.

When my older daughter graduated from High School, I joined a group of mothers who met weekly to pray for our children. Before this time, I would consider myself to be a "prayer worrier." More often than not, my prayers were asking God, "I need this," or "please do that." "Right now, Lord. I need this RIGHT NOW!" Seldom was my heart, my mind or my spirit at peace.

As I prayed with these moms, rather than approaching God with a laundry list of demands, I learned to begin my prayers with praise. I discovered that praise is not thanking God for what He has done, rather it springs from knowing who He is. Each week we focused on one attribute of God. We read the definition, then focused on scriptures from the Bible that illustrated that attribute of God's character. The more I learned about who God is, the more I found ways to praise Him. This led me to a day when God showed me how praise leads to peace.

~ Illuminating Life Lessons ~

My younger daughter would soon be a junior in high school and had struggled with math throughout her school years. The teachers, the counselor and I agreed that it would be better for her to study math one on one. Using a correspondence course for Algebra II, I became her teacher. I was willing but my student was a bit reluctant. She struggled and plodded, working every problem with me hanging over her shoulder, encouraging, explaining, and negotiating our way through the course. It felt like walking through mud with a ball and chain – for both of us!

Although she had worked every problem and turned in all the assignments, the final grade was determined only by the score on the final exam. If she failed the final exam, she failed the course. The morning she left for school to take the test we were both anxious. I remember driving by the school on my way to work, praying – pleading with God to help her remember the formulas, to help her read the questions clearly, to understand what the problem was asking, to correctly write and label the answers. As I was tearfully pleading with God, He spoke to my heart very clearly. *"Carol, don't focus on what your daughter can do, focus on what I can do."*

In that moment all of those attributes I had prayed through the years came flooding through my mind – God is faithful – God is able – God is all wisdom and knowledge – God understands - God is victorious, and on and on. Suddenly my heart was filled with praise. As I began to shift my focus to all that God is, the burden bearing down on me was lifted and replaced with a peace that Jesus describes as "beyond understanding." I knew that regardless of the outcome, everything would be OK because God is in control. As I praised God and put my hope in Him, my heart was filled with peace and joy. I shared this with my daughter and as we waited for the test results, we were able to yield the outcome to God and rest in His peace. Three weeks later when we got the test results, she had made an A on the test.

That day I learned this simple yet profound concept: "Shift your focus from what you can do to what God can do." As I learn more and more about His character through the Scriptures, my faith and trust in God grows deeper. It has changed my prayer life from being a "prayer worrier" to becoming a "prayer warrior." It has changed me from desperation and anxious thoughts to peace of heart, mind and spirit. **Isaiah 26:3 (NLT)** says it perfectly, *"You will keep in perfect peace all who trust in you, all whose thoughts are fixed on you!"*

This life changing encounter with God has given me a passion to share with others the fullness of God shown throughout the scriptures. That is the source of my peace. It is offered to you and all who will receive. It truly is the "peace that is beyond all understanding."

'O Sovereign Lord, you have only begun to show your greatness and the strength of your hand to me, your servant. Is there any god in heaven or on earth who can perform such great and mighty deeds as you do? Deuteronomy 3:24 (NLT)

Though the mountains be shaken and the hills be removed, yet my unfailing love for you will not be shaken nor my covenant of peace be removed," says the Lord, who has compassion on you. Isaiah 54:10 (NIV)

Humility

Life Lesson: I am nothing. God is everything.

In the Bible, **Numbers chapter 20** gives the account which impacted Moses severely as he led the Israelites to the promised land. Repeatedly the people complained and blamed Moses for their misery. Their constant cry was, "Why have you brought us into this wilderness to die? Why did you make us leave Egypt?" Often, they expressed a desire to return to Egypt as slaves. Their distress at times was associated with physical needs. This time they were thirsty and there was no water to drink. In verse 6, Moses and Aaron seek God and as they go to the Tabernacle, they bow face down on the ground. It was then that "the glorious presence of the Lord appeared to them." God instructs Moses to speak to a rock and He will provide the needed water. The people gather at the rock, and Moses angrily shouts, "Listen you rebels! Must we bring you water from this rock?" Then, rather than speaking to the rock, he strikes the rock. Although the needed water gushes out, with this disobedient action, Moses is doomed, never to set foot in the promised land.

As I read this passage, I feel sorry for Moses. After all, he has been given great responsibility by God and up to this point has faithfully obeyed God, even in the midst of constant complaints and great difficulty. But God's declaration to Moses stems from that one word, "we." When Moses stood before the people and struck the rock, he was putting himself in the role of the provider. In verse 12, God says to Moses and Aaron, **"Because you did not trust me enough to demonstrate my holiness to the people of Israel, you will not lead them into the land I am giving them!"**

When Moses and Aaron humbled themselves before God, His presence appeared to them. In a time of anger, the sin of pride raised its ugly head bringing about severe consequences. I have been a victim of pride, choosing to think of myself as important. I recall a day when I was teaching school that I realized, in spite of holding many responsibilities that placed me in leadership roles, when those responsibilities were given to others, I was nothing. It was a lesson in humility that I have never forgotten. It humbled me and changed me.

I remember a vivid image as I traveled home from a trip in an airplane that was humbling. As we approached the runway, I looked down and saw the landscape, the houses and buildings that appeared first as tiny specks, then grew larger as we continued down. I thought about the thousands of homes in our city, then the millions of homes all over the world, and the individuals that live in them. It helped me see that in the scope of the universe, I am as a tiny grain of sand on the beaches of all the world's oceans.

~ Illuminating Life Lessons ~

Humility is defined as a modest or low view of one's own importance. C.S. Lewis said it this way, "Humility is not thinking less of yourself, but thinking of yourself less." Such an attitude enables us to become more willing servants in God's Kingdom.

The following prayer, written long ago by a Puritan, paints a picture of humility.

> "If traces of Christ's love-artistry be upon me,
> may He work on with His divine brush
> until the complete image be obtained
> and I be made a perfect copy of Him, my Master."

Jesus was the image of humility. **And being found in human form, he humbled himself by becoming obedient to the point of death, even death on a cross.** Philippians 2:8 (ESV)

There are some who struggle with self-worth, seeking the approval of others. The more we know God, the more aware we become of our complete dependence upon Him. This results in humility as we realize that truly, we are nothing and He is everything. This realization gives us freedom from the prison of pride. May we desire to become so lost in Him that we are lost to self.

Do nothing from selfish ambition or conceit, but in humility count others more significant than yourselves.
Philippians 2:3 (ESV)

~ Illuminating Life Lessons ~

Contentment

Life Lesson: True contentment comes from within.

Contentment is being happy with what you have or who you are. If you are content, you do not desire something more or different. You are satisfied. Yet, the enemy is always lurking around the corner trying to steal our contentment and make us a slave to the world and its counterfeit pleasures. We read in **1 John 2:16 (NLT)** *"For the world offers only a craving for physical pleasure, a craving for everything we see, and pride in our achievements and possessions. These are not from the Father but are from this world."*

This verse states the three points of that are the root of all sin: the lust of the flesh, the lust of the eyes and the pride of life. Satan deceived Eve using these three points, **(Genesis 3:1-6)** just as he did when he tempted Jesus. **(Matthew 4:1-11)** Knowing that mankind could fall prey to such temptations, God included in the Ten Commandments this instruction: **Exodus 20:17 (NLT)** *"You must not covet your neighbor's house. You must not* *covet your neighbor's wife, male or female servant, ox or donkey, or anything else that belongs to your neighbor."*

Trying to "keep up with the Joneses" or to maintain a lifestyle equal or superior to others directs our focus to material things. This is part of the enemy's playbook. When we become focused on striving to attain "things," we easily lose our focus on God's blessings. The "things" that we seek never fully satisfy and always call for more and more. A friend once said, "We want things because we don't have them. Then when we get them, we don't want them anymore because we have them. And then we don't appreciate what we have so we want something else."

True satisfaction does not come from material things or physical pleasures. It does not come from high positions or worldly esteem. True satisfaction is found within the soul and comes from knowing God. This complete satisfaction allows us to acknowledge the blessings that fill our lives. It is then that we experience contentment that leads to praise.

I will praise you as long as I live, lifting up my hands to you in prayer. You satisfy me more than the richest feast. I will praise you with songs of joy. **Psalm 63:4-5 (NLT)**

The account in the scriptures of the apostle Paul is an example of living a life filled with true contentment. His story reads like an action thriller. He makes this statement in **Philippians 4:10-12 (NLT)** *"How I praise the Lord that you are concerned about me again. I know you have always been concerned for me, but you didn't have the chance to help me. Not that I was ever in need, for I have learned how to be content with whatever I have. I know how to live on almost nothing or with everything. I have*

learned the secret of living in every situation, whether it is with a full stomach or empty, with plenty or little."

In this letter to the Philippians, Paul is thanking those who have supported him. Paul says, "I have learned the secret" of being content. When did he learn this and what is the secret? In the book of Acts, we read the many situations Paul encountered as he traveled on three missionary journeys, teaching the gospel to everyone he encountered. He did not seek a receptive audience. He preached God's message of salvation everywhere he went to those who would listen as well as those who would not hear.

Paul encountered almost daily peril. Many times, angry mobs ran him out of town. He was stoned to the point of death yet continued on only to be severely beaten and thrown into prison more than once. In one town after another he faced angry mobs who threatened and ridiculed him. He was brought before high city councils, governors, kings and emperors. As a prisoner in chains, he endured a terrible storm at sea, faced death at the hands of the guards, yet survived the shipwreck and then was bitten by a poisonous snake. In the last chapter of Acts, Paul is living under guard yet still preaching the gospel.

That is what Paul did. He shared what he had experienced - the power of God through faith in Jesus Christ to transform a life. Paul's transformation was so complete, all he knew was the joy of sharing the gospel. The "secret" he learned was simple. He stated it in **Philippians 4:13 (NLT)** *"For I can do everything through Christ, who gives me strength."* He experienced that "secret" every day. True contentment does not come from wealth, power or fame. It comes from knowing God.

~ Illuminating Life Lessons ~

When I taught music at a Christian school, I wrote a musical entitled, "The Grumble Bug." It was the story of a young girl who was unhappy about almost everything. She grumbled and complained about her appearance, her family, her teachers and her friends. She was tormented within and a slave to peer pressure. Toward the end of the musical, she met a girl who had learned to be content and shared the meaning of contentment as she sang, the following lyrics.

True contentment comes from within.
It matters not the situation that I'm in.
When I think of how God loves me and my mind is stayed on Him
It doesn't matter what I wear,
If I have straight or curly hair,
Or who I'm with,
Or what I've done,
Or where I've been.
I am learning that true contentment only comes from within.
And now I'm free –
Free to be what Jesus wants me to be.
No longer a slave to the chains the world would place me in.
Yes, I am free –
He set me free.
And freely, I give my life to Him
For He alone brings contentment that comes from within.
It matters not the situation that I'm in.
When I think of how God loves me and my mind is stayed on Him.
I am learning that true contentment only comes from within.
True contentment comes from Him.

Yet true godliness with contentment is itself great wealth.
1 Timothy 6:6 (NLT)

~ Illuminating Life Lessons ~

Blessings

Life Lesson: As I am blessed, I can in turn be a blessing to others.

In our family, Thanksgiving is one of our favorite times to be together. After the meal we each share the blessings for which we are thankful. Although material blessings are sometimes mentioned, often the most heartfelt blessings are those of family, friends, and faith. I am blessed as I listen to each member of the family, from the youngest child to the oldest grandparent, relate the ways God has poured out His blessings.

God is the source of all blessing. The scriptures are filled with God's promise of blessing. Although we are undeserving, it is apparent that God enjoys blessing his children. Some blessings are conditional, but the conditions are always given to direct us in ways that will benefit us and result in blessing.

In **Matthew 5:3-11** we read the Sermon on the Mount where Jesus taught about those who are blessed. The Beatitudes are a part of that sermon and as you read this passage, it becomes clear that the character of Jesus is described. He is humble, our comforter, and righteous. He is merciful, pure and a peacemaker. He endured persecution, yet he taught that even then, blessings result from righteousness.

But God's blessings can flow through us as well as to us. God's blessings are given to us so that we may in turn bless others.

After her passing, in my mother's things I find treasures that I want to share. My mother suffered from dementia. It came on gradually – so much so that I did not realize until after her death just how long it had been overtaking her thoughts and actions. I recently found a little piece of newspaper she had saved that I wish I had seen earlier. Perhaps those who read this message will benefit if you have older parents or friends.

Beatitudes for Friends of the Aged
Blessed are they who understand my faltering step and palsied hand.
Blessed are they who seem to know that my eyes are dim, and my wits are slow.
Blessed are they who know that my ears today must strain to catch the things they say.
Blessed are they who looked away when coffee spilled at the table today.
Blessed are they with a cheery smile who stop to chat for a little while.
Blessed are thy who never say, "You've told that story twice today."
Blessed are they who know the ways to bring back memories of yesterdays.

~ Illuminating Life Lessons ~

Blessed are they who make it known that I'm loved, respected, and not alone.
Blessed are they who know I'm at a loss to find the strength to carry the Cross.
Blessed are they who ease the days on my journey Home, in loving ways.

As I read this, I thought of a special lady who visited my mother monthly for years, always listening to her stories and bringing her cookies and flowers. I remember the kind caregivers who became like family and treated her with loving care. I praise God for those who became a blessing to my mother.

God is the source of all blessing. He spoke a special blessing and instructed Moses to relay it to his people as they traveled through the wilderness. I believe God is speaking this to us today.

The LORD bless you and keep you; the LORD make his face shine on you and be gracious to you; the LORD turn his face toward you and give you peace. Numbers 6:24-26 (NIV)

~ Illuminating Life Lessons ~

Fear Not

Life Lesson: Fear holds me back from my God given potential.

Take a moment and consider the following questions. What is it that holds you back? What keeps you from stepping out into unknown territory, reaching out to others or trying a new venture? Try to condense your answer into one word. Many people I asked almost immediately gave the same answer. "Fear."

Just as so many other words in the English language, "fear" has more than one definition. First it is defined as "a feeling of alarm, terror, dread or apprehension." Surely this is not what is meant when we are commanded to fear God. The second definition of fear, however, "profound reverence and awe especially toward God" complies with the command to fear God. **Hebrews 12:28 (NLT)** illustrates this clearly: *Since we are receiving a Kingdom that is unshakable, let us be thankful and please God by worshiping him with holy fear and awe.*

All too often our experience is the fear described in **Psalm 143:3-5 (NLT)**. *My enemy has chased me.* ***He has knocked me to the ground and forces me to live in darkness like those in the grave. I am losing all hope; I am paralyzed with fear.*** How can we overcome this paralyzing fear? We find the answer in the scriptures.

The passage found in **Genesis 3:6-10** tells us that Adam and Eve enjoyed a relationship with God and were blessed with everything they needed. The fear they experienced was one of "reverence and awe." Things changed dramatically when they listened to the lies of Satan and disobeyed God. According to the scripture, their eyes were opened, and they felt shameful. They tried to hide and when God called to Adam, he responded, **"I heard you in the garden, and I was afraid..."**

When sin entered the world, fear was its companion. It has remained so until this day. The root of this dreaded emotion seems to be the issue of control. Adam and Eve took control and disobeyed God. Often the issue of control, brings about apprehension, dread, even terror. When we lose control, we often lose our peace. So, did God just leave us in this sad state of affairs? Absolutely not! Our awesome, loving God, full of grace, took control and put into motion His provision to restore the original fear that man experienced before sin entered the world – the fear that bursts forth as reverence and awe. But He asks us, just as He did Adam and Eve, to obey. We must give up control and surrender our hearts and our fears to Him. As we do, the fear of apprehension is replaced with the fear of reverence and awe. The very thing that causes fear, giving up control, is what God requires. We must trust God.

~ Illuminating Life Lessons ~

Now, fast forward to what I imagine as a still, cool, clear night in the hills around Bethlehem. The shepherds are tending their sheep. All is peaceful and quiet until suddenly in the sky there is a commotion unlike any other in all of history. The sky is illuminated, and an angel of the Lord appears. The shepherds are terrified! They are apprehensive! They are filled with fear! And what are the first words they hear from the voice of the angel? *"Fear not, for behold, I bring you good news of great joy that will be for all the people. For unto you is born this day in the city of David a Savior, who is Christ the Lord. Luke 2:10-11 (ESV)* The first words man heard when God proclaimed that we have a Savior were, **"Fear not!"**

God filled the heavens with the message that He would deliver us from our apprehension, our dread, and our terror. He set into motion the provision that would forever free us from our fears. In his love, God sent Jesus Christ, to pay the penalty for sin and restore the fellowship that was broken. As we trust God, obey Him and give up control by accepting Jesus Christ as our Savior and Lord, God delivers us from terror and apprehension. Peace is restored as we focus on our loving God with reverence and awe.

As stated in **1 John 4:18 (ESV)**, *"There is no fear in love, but perfect love casts out fear..."* As you trust in God's perfect love, remember that angelic declaration at any moment that you are alarmed or filled with terror, dread or apprehension. **Fear not!** Step out into the unknown, knowing that God will equip you to fulfill your greatest potential as you trust Him to guide you.

"For I hold you by your right hand—I, the Lord your God. And I say to you, 'Don't be afraid. I am here to help you.'"
Isaiah 41:13 (NLT)

~ Illuminating Life Lessons ~

Paradox

Life Lesson: Often in hindsight, what appears to be a paradox, is actually God's truth.

A paradox is defined as a seemingly self-contradictory statement that, when investigated or explained, is in fact true. The Bible contains some statements that are seemingly self-contradictory, yet the more we learn about God, the more we realize the truth of these statements. We read in **Isaiah 55:8-9 (ESV)**, *"My thoughts are not your thoughts, neither are your ways My ways. For as the heavens are higher than the earth, so are My ways higher than your ways and My thoughts than your thoughts."* Some examples of God's divine logic include the following scriptures.

Galatians 2:20a (KJV) I am crucified with Christ: nevertheless, I live; yet not I, but Christ liveth in me.

Luke 17:33 (ESV) Whoever seeks to preserve his life will lose it, but whoever loses his life will keep it.

1 Corinthians 3:18 (NLT) Stop deceiving yourselves. If you think you are wise by this world's standards, you need to become a fool to be truly wise.

Matthew 23:12 (NLT) But those who exalt themselves will be humbled, and those who humble themselves will be exalted.

Matthew 20:16 (NLT) So those who are last now will be first then, and those who are first will be last.

Matthew 23:11(ESV) The greatest among you shall be your servant.

2 Corinthians 12:10 (NLT) That's why I take pleasure in my weaknesses, and in the insults, hardships, persecutions, and troubles that I suffer for Christ. For when I am weak, then I am strong.

Proverbs 11:24 (NLT) Give freely and become more wealthy; be stingy and lose everything.

James 1:2-3 (ESV) Count it all joy, my brothers, when you meet trials of various kinds, for you know that the testing of your faith produces steadfastness

To some, the paradoxical statements in the Bible may seem absurd. We find life by losing it. To be first we must be last. Trials in life are counted as joy. When we are weak, we are strong. At times, in life, we experience circumstances that we simply do not understand. We face a paradox. Yet, in God's timing, and usually in hindsight, we begin to see God's purposes revealed. Our lack of complete understanding of these paradoxes becomes clearer the more we know about God through His Word. As the Holy Spirit teaches God's truth, we experience a deeper understanding of God.

In **1 Corinthians 13:12 (NLT)** we read, *"Now we see things imperfectly, like puzzling reflections in a mirror, but then we will see everything with perfect clarity. All that I know now is partial and incomplete, but then I will know everything completely, just as God now knows me completely."*

I have been reading about the history of the Pilgrims as they traveled across the ocean in a crowded ship, facing the perils of disease and hardship. In the book *The Valley of Vision: A Collection of Puritan Prayers and Devotions,* edited by Arthur Bennett, I found this prayer which is rephrased for clarity.

> Lord high and holy, meek and lowly,
> You have brought me to the valley of vision,
> where I live in the deep, but see You in the heights;
> hemmed in by mountains of sin, I see Your glory.
> Let me learn by paradox
> That the way down is the way up,
> That to be low is to be high,
> That the broken heart is the healed heart,
> That the contrite spirit is the joyful spirit,
> That the remorseful soul is the victorious soul,
> That to have nothing is to possess it all,
> That to bear the cross is to wear the crown,
> That to give is to receive,
> That the valley is the place of vision.
> Lord in the daytime, stars can be seen in the deepest wells,
> And the deeper the wells, the brighter the stars shine;

Let me find Your light in my darkness,
Your life in my death,
Your joy in my sorrow,
Your grace in my sin,
Your riches in my poverty
Your glory in my valley.

If you are facing a situation that seems like a paradox, ask yourself, "What is God teaching me?" This very situation may lead you to a peace, joy, rest or victory that demonstrates God's enduring love for you.

Oh, the depth of the riches and wisdom and knowledge of God! How unsearchable are His judgments and how unfathomable His ways. Romans 11:33 (NLT)

Success

Life Lesson: Your success will be determined by how determined you are to succeed.

Success can be defined in many ways. To some it may be a measure of prosperity, affluence or comfort. To others it might be a victory or favorable outcome. I look at success as the accomplishment of a goal or purpose.

As a teacher, my desire for all my students was for them to experience success. This was challenging for some, for the subject I taught was Chemistry. Every year I would hear the same lament, "Why do we have to learn Chemistry!?" I tried to explain that the study of Chemistry would help them as they faced the problems of life. Many of the problems they were given to solve required several steps to find the correct answer. All too often, the students wanted the solution to be simple and obvious. The problems and challenges in life are not that simple. Some require time and determination to work hard and never give up until success is achieved.

I remember one student in particular who had no interest in Chemistry but had a strong desire to succeed. This student faced learning differences that required extra time, both on the student's part and mine. As we worked together, I saw how hard this student worked trying to master the concepts. Her diligence and perseverance were rewarded with an A at the end of the course. Others who put forth little effort received lesser grades.

I was required to take a course in Educational Psychology as a part of my accreditation requirements. In that class I learned a concept that I shared with my students. I have shared it with many parents as well and it is so impactful, I am compelled to share it to illustrate this life lesson.

As we look toward the accomplishment of a goal or purpose, we are affected by two types of factors. **Extrinsic factors** are those that are not part of the essential nature of someone or something; coming or operating from the outside. These factors are beyond our control. **Intrinsic factors** are the second type of factors which belong to the essential nature of someone or something; inborn; innate, natural.

When seeking to achieve success, we must consider the motivation of the individual. Motivation is simply what causes you to act. When we associate the extrinsic and intrinsic factors with motivation, we begin to see a revelation that can be life changing when applied. Let's consider a student taking a test or perhaps an adult with a particular challenge.

The two extrinsic factors are 1. test or challenge and 2. luck. A person has no control over the test or the challenge they face. It will not change. They simply must face it head on. They may depend on luck to help them get the right answer on the test or to overcome the challenge, but luck is only a matter of chance. It is a fickle companion. Wishing for luck will have no effect upon the success or failure of the individual.

The two intrinsic factors are 1. ability and 2. effort. These are factors which are a part of a person's nature. One factor, ability, is something that we are born with. Our abilities vary with each individual. Some have abilities in mathematics and science, others have abilities in language or art or music. The abilities we have are our God given abilities. They can be used for His purposes to bring glory to God, but the natural abilities are just that, a part of our nature. The second intrinsic factor is effort which is defined as a vigorous, determined attempt. Effort, to put it simply, is just working hard.

As we look at these factors, the test or challenge, luck, ability and effort, there is only one that we control. Effort. In order to succeed, we must stop trying to change the test, forget depending upon luck, stop complaining that we aren't smart enough and just start working hard. That is the path to success.

There is one other factor that we should consider and that is God. When we are faced with difficulties, while applying our effort, we can draw on God's power to help us.

In the scriptures we read about the life of Paul who faced one challenge after another. Yet He records in his letter to the Corinthians that God spoke to him when he was faced with something that he could not control. God said to Paul, *"My grace is sufficient for you, for my power is made perfect in weakness."* **2 Corinthians 12:9a. (ESV)** Then in his letter to the Philippians

Paul declared, *"For I can do everything through Christ, who gives me strength."* **Philippians 4:13 (NLT)**

The one conclusion that can lead to success –
work hard and trust God.

Let us, your servants, see you work again; let our children see your glory. And may the Lord our God show us his approval and make our efforts successful. Yes, make our efforts successful! Psalm 90:16-17 (NLT)

Yours, O Lord, is the greatness, the power, the glory, the victory, and the majesty. Everything in the heavens and on earth is yours, O Lord, and this is your kingdom. We adore you as the one who is over all things. Wealth and honor come from you alone, for you rule over everything. Power and might are in your hand, and at your discretion people are made great and given strength. 1 Chronicles 29:11-12 (NLT)

~ Illuminating Life Lessons ~

God is Resolute

Life Lesson: When God says, "I will," He does.

Perhaps you are aware of the trend to choose a word for the new year. Recently I heard a spin on that trend. Some say there is a word we must remove from our vocabulary. What is that word? It is "should." Rather than saying, "I should do this or that," we must replace it with "I will…" As we begin a new year, often we make resolutions. Perhaps we resolve to lose weight or start an exercise program. There are resolutions concerning health, family, work, faith and on and on. Sadly, those resolutions may be forgotten as quickly as they are made. Our problem - we are not resolute. We lack the unwavering determination to see our resolutions fulfilled.

The scriptures are filled with resolutions that God has made to His children. God does not use the word "should" when He makes His promises. How could we trust God if His promises were prefaced with "I should?" When God makes a promise and says, "I will," He does. He resolves to keep His covenant of love and all that such a covenant encompasses – love, protection, salvation, forgiveness, faithfulness, rest, guidance and peace.

God said to Noah, *"I will confirm my covenant with you."* **Genesis 6:18 (NLT)**

To Abraham He said, *"I will always be your God and the God of your descendants after you."* **Genesis 17:7 (NLT)**

He made this promise to Jacob, *"I will protect you wherever you go… I will not leave you until I have finished giving you everything I have promised you."* **Genesis 28:15 (NLT)**

To Moses He promised, *"I will free you from your oppression and will rescue you from your slavery in Egypt. I will redeem you with a powerful arm and great acts of judgment." **Exodus 6:6 (NLT)***

And to Solomon, God said, *"Because your greatest desire is to help your people… I will certainly give you the wisdom and knowledge you requested. But I will also give you wealth, riches, and fame such as no other king has had before you or will ever have in the future!"* **2 Chronicles 1:11-12 (NLT)**

These are some of the **"I will"** promises He gives to us:

The LORD says, *"I will guide you along the best pathway for your life. I will advise and watch over you."* **Psalm 32:8 (NLT)**

~ Illuminating Life Lessons ~

The LORD says, *"I will rescue those who love me. I will protect those who trust in my name. When they call on me, I will answer; I will be with them in trouble. I will rescue and honor them. I will reward them with a long life and give them my salvation."* Psalm 91:14-16 (NLT)

"Come now, let's settle this," says the LORD. *"Though your sins are like scarlet, I will make them as white as snow. Though they are red like crimson, I will make them as white as wool."* Isaiah 1:18 (NLT)

"I will be your God throughout your lifetime—until your hair is white with age. I made you, and I will care for you. I will carry you along and save you." Isaiah 46:4 (NLT)

Jesus said, *"Come to me, all of you who are weary and carry heavy burdens, and I will give you rest."* Matthew 11:28 (NLT)

Perhaps you have made some resolutions. Rather than saying, "I should," shift your focus from what you can do to what God can do. With God's help say, "I will!" God's fixed, firm purpose is to fill our lives with His fullness. I praise God for He is resolute.

...O Lord, you are a great and awesome God! You always fulfill your covenant and keep your promises of unfailing love to those who love you and obey your commands.
Daniel 9:4 (NLT)

I trust in God, so why should I be afraid? What can mere mortals do to me? I will fulfill my vows to you, O God, and will offer a sacrifice of thanks for your help. Psalm 56:11-12 (NLT)

God Makes Things New

Life Lesson: I will let go of past burdens and rest in the promise that God makes all things new.

As we begin each new year, often we resolve to do some things differently. All too often, our resolve weakens as the days go on and we find ourselves settling back into our old habits. There is a passage in **Revelation 21:1-5 (NKJV)** that reveals God's resolve to us. The Apostle John wrote, *"Now I saw a new heaven and a new earth, for the first heaven and the first earth had passed away. Also. there was no more sea. Then I, John, saw the holy city, New Jerusalem, coming down out of heaven from God, prepared as a bride adorned for her husband. And I heard a loud voice from heaven saying, "Behold, the tabernacle of God is with men, and He will dwell with them, and they shall be His people. God Himself will be with them and be their God. And God will wipe away every tear from their eyes; there shall be no more death, nor sorrow, nor crying. There shall be no more pain, for the former things have passed away." Then He who sat on the throne said, "Behold, I make all things new." And He said to me, "Write, for these words are true and faithful."*

God's Word is our faithful source of truth. The following are just a few of His promises:

New creation - Isaiah 65:17-18a (NLT) *"Look! I am creating new heavens and a new earth, and no one will even think about the old ones anymore. Be glad; rejoice forever in my creation!"*

New covenant - Luke 22:20 (NLT) *After supper He took another cup of wine and said, "This cup is the new covenant between God and his people—an agreement confirmed with my blood, which is poured out as a sacrifice for you."*

New mercies every morning - Lamentations 3:22-24 (ESV) *The steadfast love of the L*ORD *never ceases; his mercies never come to an end; they are new every morning; great is your faithfulness. "The L*ORD *is my portion," says my soul, "therefore I will hope in him."*

New things new ways - Isaiah 43:18,19 (NIV) *"Forget the former things; do not dwell on the past. See, I am doing a new thing! Now it springs up; do you not perceive it? I am making a way in the desert and streams in the wasteland."*

New life - 2 Corinthians 5:17 (NLT) *This means that anyone who belongs to Christ has become a new person. The old life is gone; a new life has begun!*

New song - Psalm 40:3 (NLT) *He has given me a new song to sing, a hymn of praise to our God. Many will see what he has done and be amazed. They will put their trust in the L*ORD.

New heart - Ezekiel 36:26 (NLT) *And I will give you a new heart, and I will put a new spirit in you. I will take out your stony, stubborn heart and give you a tender, responsive heart.*

New freedom - Hebrews 9:14b-15 (NLT) *For by the power of the eternal Spirit, Christ offered himself to God as a perfect sacrifice for our sins. That is why he is the one who mediates a new covenant between God and people, so that all who are called can receive the eternal inheritance God has promised them. For Christ died to set them free from the penalty of the sins they had committed under that first covenant.*

So often it is those "former things" that cause us sorrow or regret. But God reveals in His Word that He is faithful to make things new. Starting now, let us let go of the former things and cling to God's faithful and true message to us that God makes things different from that which has been before. God makes things new.

So, we're not giving up. How could we! Even though on the outside it often looks like things are falling apart on us, on the inside, where God is making new life, not a day goes by without his unfolding grace. These hard times are small potatoes compared to the coming good times; the lavish celebration prepared for us. There's far more here than meets the eye. The things we see now are here today, gone tomorrow. But the things we can't see now will last forever. **2 Corinthians 4:16-18 (MSG)**

~ Illuminating Life Lessons ~

~ Illuminating Life Lessons ~

Control

Life Lesson: I must surrender in order to allow God to take control.

Several years ago, I was invited to be a part of a panel for a presentation to young mothers. One question directed to me was, "What phase of motherhood is the most difficult?" Many thoughts rushed through my mind but almost immediately I found the answer. I replied, "I don't think there is any one phase that is the most difficult, it is the transition times between phases that are the most difficult."

That brings up the issue of control. Have you ever considered why the word "expecting" is used to indicate that a baby is on the way? Perhaps, as it was in my experience, it is because the moment that you find out that you are going to have a child, you are filled with all sorts of expectations. In reality, our "expectations" simply set us up for situations that we never "expected." Some of these situations lead to disappointment, fear and pain. As our child transitions from infant to toddler, from pre-school to elementary school, and from pre-teen to teenager

~ Illuminating Life Lessons ~

to adult, with each change, we must give up more and more control. For a mother who wants to love and protect her child, this is a very difficult thing to do.

These transition times can be frustrating and challenging for both child and mother. The day eventually comes when you have no control. Even though you want to offer all sorts of good advice, to try to fix and rescue and help, it becomes clear that your child will not learn from your experience. They will only learn from their own. At that point, what can a mother do?

I found the answer when my older daughter graduated from high school and entered college. It was then that I was invited to join a Moms in Prayer group. We met weekly to pray for our children and schools. To say that my life was transformed is an understatement. It changed me from a "prayer worrier" to a "prayer warrior." I learned to pray in a new way. Rather than just giving God a laundry-list of things I wanted Him to do, I learned to praise Him for who He is. I learned that praise is not thanking Him for what He has done but it springs from knowing His character. Each week we focused on one of the attributes of God and after reading scripture that illustrated that attribute, we spent some time just praising Him. We then had a time of silent confession, then a time of acknowledging and thanking God for the ways we see Him at work in response to our prayers.

You may notice that up to this point in our prayer time we had not asked for anything. Our entire focus was on God – praising Him, seeking His forgiveness, and thanking Him. Now we were ready to bring our cares and concerns to Him, trusting in His power and His faithfulness.

After 24 years, I still meet with moms and pray with them in this way. Learning four simple steps of prayer has filled my life with passion and purpose. These four steps can be remembered by the word "**PRAY.**" **Praise – Repent - Acknowledge – Yield.** My life has been transformed as I have learned to shift my focus from what I can do to what God can do. This changes my perspective, for I am trusting the One who is faithful to work in ways that will give me peace and bring Him glory.

Some time ago while I was babysitting my grandson, he became tired and distressed. He was crying, resisting my efforts to calm him. Finally, he came to me and raised up his arms. It was as though he was saying, "I surrender. Take me in your arms and hold me." I bent down to him, lifted him into my arms and held him until he was comforted. Yet, before I could do this, he first had to give up control.

This reminded me that when I surrender and give up control to God, I find peace, that rest of heart, mind and spirit that we all seek. This peace is based on the fact that God is in control, God is sovereign, God has a plan, and God is always at work – regardless of what it might look like at the moment. A mom at peace is a much better mom. She is not striving – she is resting.

My help comes from the LORD**, who made heaven and earth!**
Psalm 121:2 (NLT)

~ Illuminating Life Lessons ~

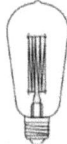

Trust

Life Lesson: If I can trust imperfect mankind, why would I not trust perfect God?

Have you ever taken a trust fall? It is when you stand on a platform and below you are people with their arms extended in order to catch you before you hit the ground as you fall backwards. It requires a great deal of trust. You must trust people that you may not even know. You must trust that they are strong enough to hold you. You must trust that they will protect you from harm.

In San Antonio, as in many cities, a huge interchange with multiple high ramps is being built in a very busy area. I was passing by recently and as I looked at the unfinished ramps, I thought about all the workers who had a part in their construction. There were engineers who had to calculate carefully and make blueprints that others would precisely follow. There were those who built the steel beams and mixed the concrete. Others constructed the forms and secured the beams. There were hundreds of people involved in the construction.

There will be millions of times that drivers will travel on these ramps with total trust that they are secure. This is just one example, but our lives are filled with all sorts of instances when we blindly trust all of those who affect our lives.

The opposite of trust is doubt. Where trust fills you with confidence and peace, doubt fills you with questions. We all have questions at one time or another which is only an indication that we have faith. You cannot doubt something that you do not have. But often accompanying doubt is fear. We have an enemy, Satan, who weaponizes doubt, causing us to be paralyzed with fear. Like a thief, Satan tries to steal our peace as stated in **John 10:10, (NASB)** *"The thief comes only to steal and kill and destroy."* But Jesus goes on to say, *"I came that they may have life, and have it abundantly."*

The remedy for fear is to trust God. Some would ask, "How can I learn to trust God?" This is difficult if God is a stranger to you. But just as you would take time and effort learning to trust a friend, you must spend time getting to know about God's character and attributes. The Bible gives us a clear picture of a loving God who simply would not give up on us. God is worthy of our trust because He never lies and never fails to fulfill His promises. He proves Himself to be trustworthy in our lives and the lives of others. What alternative do we have? Would we trust in ourselves, in others who are unreliable and have limited wisdom, or the all-wise, all-knowing, all-powerful, gracious, merciful, loving God who wants good things for us? The choice should be obvious, but we must seek to know Him.

Who is God to you? Is He big or small? Is He strong? Is He wise? Does He love you? Seek God. Know who He is. The more you know Him, the greater will be your trust in Him.

If we can trust man – full of imperfections, how much more can we trust God. Do you believe that God is completely trustworthy? Is this something you profess, yet find yourself filled with fear and turmoil? It is easy for us to say that we **trust in** God, but **don't just trust in God, trust God!** Take a trust fall, let go and put all your doubts and fears in the capable hands of God. God is trustworthy!

I pray that God, the source of hope, will fill you completely with joy and peace because you trust in him. Then you will overflow with confident hope through the power of the Holy Spirit. Romans 15:13 (NLT)

~ Illuminating Life Lessons ~

~ Illuminating Life Lessons ~

Consider the Cost

Life Lesson: God offers salvation as a free gift, though the cost of it was great.

After a holiday like Christmas, many find themselves closely checking their bank account balance as the bills come in. The costs vary but usually include decorations, food, travel and gifts. Although many sacrifice to cover the costs, most would agree that the joy that accompanies the sacrifice is well worth the cost. When we consider the birth of Jesus Christ, there were no decorations, little food, difficult travel, but one priceless gift that was accompanied by great sacrifice and great cost. Consider the following based on a Christmas Meditation that a friend shared with me.

Jesus left the right hand of the father, the seat of glory honor and power to come and live among us on this broken planet. He was the center of worship and praise in heaven and creator of all things. Yet He set aside being the One sought by heavenly beings for wisdom to become a baby who could not speak. The very Word of God became silent except for His crying.

~ Illuminating Life Lessons ~

The radiance of Jesus, who was clothed in glory and illuminated the heavens, humbly became swaddled in a blanket by his mother to keep warm.

Jesus willingly exchanged His throne of glory, surrounded in splendor and the sound of the heavenly chorus declaring, "Holy, holy, holy is the Lord God Almighty," for a bed of straw in a feeding trough accompanied by flies and the choir of farm animals wailing out in the night.

Jesus abandoned His role as the Giver of Life and assumed the role of a helpless baby at the mercy of others for survival.

Jesus, who ruled heaven in righteousness, submitted Himself to the pain and shame of a world ruled by unrighteous men. The very Son of God was mocked and disgraced for His lack of parentage. He suffered the humiliation of a poor family which couldn't afford a lamb for the purification, but sacrificed the poor man's offering of two doves.

Jesus, the Prince of Peace, who came to bring life to all, suffered great humiliation and shame in coming. He was welcomed into the world by a few unclean foreigners and some despised shepherds of Israel, not by the coronation of the King of Kings.

From the very beginning, Jesus came in shame to bring us into His glory, and to make those who were once vessels of shame into vessels of honor.
Great was the cost Jesus paid to bring to us the gifts of peace, joy, hope, love and eternal life with Him in glory.

Jesus knew the cost before He came. As He considered the cost, He did not hesitate to pay in full as He shed His blood on the cross.
Jesus stooped to the death of the worst kind of criminal to take our shame and sin.

Though he was God, He did not think of equality with God as something to cling to. Instead, He gave up his divine privileges; He took the humble position of a slave and was born as a human being. When he appeared in human form, he humbled himself in obedience to God and died a criminal's death on a cross. Philippians 2:6-8 (NLT)

As we reflect upon the true meaning of Christmas, let us not only celebrate the birth of our Savior, but let us consider the cost.

**Therefore, since we are surrounded by such a huge crowd of witnesses to the life of faith, let us strip off every weight that slows us down, especially the sin that so easily trips us up. And let us run with endurance the race God has set before us. We do this by keeping our eyes on Jesus, the champion who initiates and perfects our faith. Because of the joy awaiting him, he endured the cross, disregarding its shame. Now he is seated in the place of honor beside God's throne.
Hebrews 12:1-2 (NLT)**

~ Illuminating Life Lessons ~

The Mediator

Life Lesson: Jesus Christ is the mediator between God and man and God entrusts to me the message of reconciliation.

According to the dictionary, a mediator is one that works to effect reconciliation between parties at variance; a peacemaker or a go-between. To reconcile means to make friendly again; to settle a difference; to make compatible and to bring into harmony.

The account in the Bible of the life of Job reveals a man who experiences extreme loss. As I was reading the book of Job this passage caught my attention: *"God is not a mortal like me, so I cannot argue with him or take him to trial. If only there were a mediator between us, someone who could bring us together. The mediator could make God stop beating me, and I would no longer live in terror of his punishment." Job 9:32-34 (NLT)* Here Job recognizes the greatness, the power and the authority of God. In his despair he longs for a mediator - someone to plead his case. Someone to bring back the peace he had once known.

The moment I read the word "mediator" I realized that God had one in place from the beginning. God made this provision as stated in **John 1:1-2,14 (NLT)**. *"In the beginning the Word already existed. The Word was with God, and the Word was God. He existed in the beginning with God. So, the Word became human and made his home among us. He was full of unfailing love and faithfulness. And we have seen his glory, the glory of the Father's one and only Son."* As our peacemaker, Jesus stretched out His hands as they were nailed to the cross. With one hand He held the hand of God and with the other He held the hand of mankind. His shed blood fulfilled the justice God demands for our sin and through Him, we are reconciled. When we acknowledge that it is His sacrifice that closes the chasm between ourselves and God, and receive it personally, our relationship is reconciled, and we become friends with God. Jesus Christ is our mediator.

And there is more. In **2 Corinthians 5:17-19 (NLT)** we read *"This means that anyone who belongs to Christ has become a new person. The old life is gone; a new life has begun! And all of this is a gift from God, who brought us back to himself through Christ. And God has given us this task of reconciling people to him. For God was in Christ, reconciling the world to himself, no longer counting people's sins against them. And he gave us this wonderful message of reconciliation."*

Have you ever received good news or perhaps a gift that brought such joy you simply couldn't contain it? It is human nature to want to share unexpected joy. Yet what greater joy could there be than the joy of our salvation? In the verse above we are given a task. We have the privilege to share the "wonderful message of reconciliation."

This message is very simple. **In John 14:6 (NLT)** Jesus says, *"I am the way, the truth and the life. No one can come to the Father except through me."* To some this might be considered "narrow-minded," however, one can also see it as God's specific message through His Word to assure that we know the path to the salvation. The enemy would like to confuse that message with alternative paths. It has been said, "Truth is narrow. Lies will take you in many different directions." God's word is exact and He clearly shows us how to establish fellowship with Him.

Every day we encounter those who are seeking purpose and peace. Resolve to tell someone about the One Mediator who offers peace between God and man. Experience the unspeakable joy as you see them shed the burden of sin and put on the salvation of God.

There is one God and one Mediator who can reconcile God and humanity—the man Christ Jesus. 1 Timothy 2:5 (NLT)

~ Illuminating Life Lessons ~

What's in a Name?

Life Lesson: There is power in the name of Jesus Christ.

I saw a man being interviewed on the news who had rescued a person from a burning car. The victim was trapped, and others had tried to help, but were unsuccessful. When asked how this man was able to pull the person out to safety, he responded, "I spoke the name of Jesus and immediately was able to pull the person to safety."

The scriptures reveal that God chose the name for His Son. In **Matthew 1:20-22 (NLT)** we read that an angel of the Lord appeared to Joseph in a dream and told him that Mary would have a son. *"You are to name him Jesus, for he will save his people from their sins."* Although some might think of "Christ" as Jesus' last name, it actually comes from the Greek word *Christos* meaning "anointed one" or "chosen one." This is the Greek equivalent of the Hebrew word *Mashiach*, or "Messiah." So "Christ" is his title, signifying Jesus was sent from God to be a King and Deliverer. Jesus' birth was prophesied by Isaiah almost 700 years before Jesus was born. In his prophecy we read from **Isaiah 9:6 (NLT)** *"For a child is born to us, a son is given to us. The government will rest on his shoulders. And he will be called: Wonderful Counselor, Mighty God, Everlasting Father, Prince of Peace."*

Jesus Christ is the fulfillment of this prophecy as we see in the Scriptures.

Wonderful - *So just as sin ruled over all people and brought them to death, now God's wonderful grace rules instead, giving us right standing with God and resulting in eternal life through Jesus Christ our Lord.* **Romans 5:21 (NLT)**

Counselor – *I will instruct you and teach you in the way you should go; I will counsel you with my loving eye on you.* **Psalm 32:8 (NIV)**

Not only is Jesus Christ the anointed one – the Messiah – the Wonderful Counselor, He is Mighty God. Jesus is the Spirit of God in human flesh. Although Jesus faced the same human experiences we do, He had power that we do not. He carefully and wisely chose how to use that power in ways that would bring glory to God.

Mighty God - *For the Lord your God is living among you. He is a mighty savior. He will take delight in you with gladness. With his love, he will calm all your fears. He will rejoice over you with joyful songs.* **Zephaniah 3:17 (NLT)**

Another prophecy Isaiah spoke about Jesus is that He is Everlasting Father. The thought of something being everlasting is difficult to comprehend, especially in our increasingly "disposable" society. Again, in the scriptures we read of God's everlasting love, everlasting righteousness, and everlasting kindness. He is our everlasting light and through faith in him, we are given everlasting life.

Everlasting Father - *Do you not know? Have you not heard? The LORD is the everlasting God, the Creator of the ends of the earth. He will not grow tired or weary, and his understanding no one can fathom.* Isaiah 40:28 (NIV)

Peace comes from God. Just as He offers us the gift of salvation, He gives us the gift of peace. That gift came in the form of the Prince of Peace, Jesus Christ. This peace is not of the world – not an artificial peace that is dependent upon our worthiness or our circumstance. It is a peace that exceeds anything we can understand. It is a peace that guards our hearts. It is true peace – true rest of spirit, mind and body. Jesus speaks this peace to us over and over again in the scriptures.

Prince of Peace - *I am leaving you with a gift—peace of mind and heart. And the peace I give is a gift the world cannot give. So, don't be troubled or afraid.* John 14:27 (NLT)

The Christmas holiday can become a time of focusing on decorating, cooking, shopping and preparing for a day with family and friends. Perhaps you have family traditions that have endured through the years. Our family tradition started over 30 years ago. My young daughter suggested that we build a manger from some leftover fence wood and stage a live nativity scene in our front yard on Christmas eve. Through the years we have added family members, spouses of our children, our grandchildren, even in-laws as we dress as shepherds and wise men, Mary and Joseph, and an angel. We quietly focus on the baby Jesus as worshipful music plays. Many drive slowly by, others walk to our home, and focus on the true meaning of Christmas. Our prayer is that they will come to personally know

Jesus Christ the Messiah – Wonderful Counselor, Mighty God, Everlasting Father, Prince of Peace.

In John 20:31 (NLT) we read, *"But these are written so that you may continue to believe that Jesus is the Messiah, the Son of God, and that by believing in him you will have life by the power of his name."* Not only do we discover in the life of Jesus the fulfillment of prophesy, the scriptures reveal the power of the name of Jesus.

We pray in the name of Jesus for He is the way that we come into a relationship with God. It is because of Jesus that we can come before the presence of God in prayer. Jesus told His disciples, ***"Truly, truly, I say to you, whatever you ask of the Father in my name, he will give it to you. Until now you have asked nothing in my name. Ask, and you will receive, that your joy may be full."* John 16:23b-24 (ESV).** When we pray according to the will of God, trusting in His timing and for the glory of God, we experience the power of the name of Jesus.

There is salvation in the name of Jesus. *"For Jesus is the one referred to in the Scriptures, where it says, 'The stone that you builders rejected has now become the cornerstone.' There is salvation in no one else! God has given no other name under heaven by which we must be saved.* **"Acts 4:11-12 (NLT)**

What's in a name? In the name of Jesus Christ there is salvation, forgiveness, love, hope, power, victory, rest and peace.

~ Illuminating Life Lessons ~

Therefore, God elevated him to the place of highest honor and gave him the name above all other names, that at the name of Jesus every knee should bow, in heaven and on earth and under the earth, and every tongue declare that Jesus Christ is Lord, to the glory of God the Father. Philippians 2:9-11 (NLT)

~ Illuminating Life Lessons ~

~ Illuminating Life Lessons ~

Empty Spaces in Life's Journey

Life Lesson: The journey of life is peaceful when I trust God to fill the empty spaces.

What a blessing, as we travel down the road of life, to know that we are not alone. Not only is God near, He is able to meet every need that we face. Those empty spaces that appear as we take our journey, like potholes in a road, need not become deep and dangerous. As we focus on God and all that He is, those empty spaces are filled with His fullness and our journey is safe and peaceful.

As we focus on how God fills the empty spaces in the journey of life, we see that **God is accessible**, available every moment that we have a need. When we question the purpose of our journey, **God anoints** us with a special plan. As we surrender to him, **God is our authority,** and he protects us and frees us from the threat of the enemy. When things seem to be crumbling around us, **God builds** and develops a mature faith as we trust in him. **God gives commands** that direct our path to safety and blessing. When we take a wrong turn, **God corrects** our path giving us clear direction.

If we become lost, **God is our counselor**, and he instructs us in the way we should go. **God delivers** us when the things of the world would hijack us.

When we become weary, we find that **God is enough** to help us continue on. When we are faced with uncertainty, **God establishes** order and stabilizes our thoughts. **God is our example** through the life of Christ and inspires us to respond in love and obedience. Though we may not have worldly riches, **God is extravagant,** and his provision and love fills our journey with joy beyond measure. He does not leave us in the middle of our journey, but **God finishes** with us. When we need to rebuild the road in our journey, **God is the foundation** and the solid rock in our life*.*

God gives grace when we are helpless, and we are encouraged. We are surrounded by the wonders of his creation and we see that **God is great. God guards** us so that we need not be anxious about anything. If we are distressed and call for help, **God hears**. When we need a place to rest, **God is our hiding place. God values humility** and when we yield to him, he saves us, guiding and teaching us the way we should go. In the darkness, **God illuminates** our path. **God is impartial** giving direction to all who call upon him. When the journey seems long and hard, **God inspires** us to continue on.

When we are confused and need direction, **God intercedes**. When we make a mistake, **God judges** with righteousness and justice and disciplines those he loves. **God keeps** in perfect peace all who trust in him and maintain their focus on him. **God knows** of any roadblocks we may face. As he fills our journey with joy, **God gives laughter.** When we thirst, **God is the spring of living**

water. As we witness the splendor of his creation, we see that ***God is majestic.*** ***God overcomes*** any obstacle that blocks our way. He is aware of every traveler and knows every journey for ***God is personal.*** Our journey has meaning because ***God is purposeful.*** Although wrong decisions may enslave us, ***God redeems*** our life.

God reigns over all the earth enduring throughout all generations. When we grow tired and weary, ***God renews*** our strength and ***God gives rest.*** Even when we suffer loss, ***God restores.*** When we must make decisions that affect our journey, ***God reveals*** truth. ***God remains the same*** and we can always depend on his faithfulness. When we are faced with danger or harm, ***God saves.*** When we face uncertainty and feel anxious, ***God secures.*** Nothing we face is too difficult for him, for ***God is sovereign.***

When weakness overcomes us, ***God is our strength.*** When the journey is tiresome and we feel that we cannot go on, ***God sustains.*** In the midst of storms ***God transforms*** the conditions and we enjoy pleasant travel. No matter what our doubts or how great our confusion, ***God understands.*** If fear overtakes us, ***God upholds*** keeping us safe and calm. He is aware of all that we encounter for ***God watches*** us, protecting and guarding as we go. If we find that we are in the midst of difficulties that overwhelm us, we can be confident, for ***God is with us.*** As we continue our journey, ***God works*** all things for good and conforms our life to be more like his Son. Because he demonstrates over and over throughout our journey that he is unequalled and faithful in every way, ***God is worthy*** of our praise.

May you be blessed as you keep God ***fully in focus.***

~ Illuminating Life Lessons ~

**You will keep in perfect peace
All who trust in You –
All whose thoughts are
Fixed (focused) on You.
Isaiah 26:3 (NLT)**

God Finishes

Life Lesson: Until the day when Jesus returns and His work is finished, God is at work in me and God can work through me.

The Scriptures reveal that God does not stop His work until it is finished. In **Genesis 2:2 (NLT)** we read. *"On the seventh day God had finished his work of creation, so he rested from all his work."* Every speck of creation was finished. God reveals His works to us as He equips us to discover more of His creation, but it has all been there since God put on His finishing touches. Not only did God finish His creation, He finishes His work in us. In **Philippians 1:6 (NLT)** we read, *"And I am certain that God, who began the good work within you, will continue his work until it is finally finished on the day when Christ Jesus returns."*

I will never forget watching a long-distance race one Olympic season when one of the last runners collapsed on the track. The crowd became silent as they watched the runner struggle to stand, obviously overcome with exhaustion and defeat. It was at that moment that a man bounded onto the track and ran toward the runner. I thought perhaps it was medical personnel coming to assist the runner to ensure his safety. As the man approached the runner, it became obvious that he was not there to give him medical attention. The man was the runner's father. As he arrived at the place where his son lay, he gently took his hand, pulling him up placing his son's arm over his shoulder. Bearing the weight of his son, they haltingly walked to the finish line.

This evokes a beautiful picture of God our Father and His gift of salvation. Although mankind was lost and defeated by sin, God completed His work to reconcile a relationship with man. Jesus, hanging on the cross, cried out, **"It is finished."** Victory over sin is complete as God's offers the power of His love to save us.

We read in **2 Corinthians 5:17-19 (NLT)** *This means that anyone who belongs to Christ has become a new person. The old life is gone; a new life has begun! And all of this is a gift from God, who brought us back to himself through Christ. And God has given us this task of reconciling people to him. For God was in Christ, reconciling the world to himself, no longer counting people's sins against them. And he gave us this wonderful message of reconciliation.*

Now we, too, have work that needs to be finished. In his book, *Tell Someone*, author Greg Laurie states that although every Christian wants to lead others to Christ, where we fall short is in closing the deal. Although we are willing to share our salvation experience, we are hesitant to finish and ask that very important question, **"Would you like to ask Jesus Christ into your life right now?"**

And even then, our work is not complete. When Jesus had finished His work on earth, He told His disciples, *"I have been given all authority in heaven and on earth. Therefore, go and make disciples of all the nations, baptizing them in the name of the Father and the Son and the Holy Spirit. Teach these new disciples to obey all the commands I have given you. And be sure of this: I am with you always, even to the end of the age."*
Matthew 28:18-20 (NLT)

This is the work that God has given us –to share the message of reconciliation and to make disciples. Jesus tells us to disciple those He brings into our life with the assurance that He will equip us and always – even to the end of the age – be with us. Let us yield ourselves to God and finish our work.

God finished creation, He finished salvation on the cross and He finishes His work in us. From the beginning to the end, God finishes.

**And he also said, "It is finished!
I am the Alpha and the Omega—the Beginning and the End.
To all who are thirsty I will give freely
from the springs of the water of life.
Revelation 21:6 (NLT)**

~ Illuminating Life Lessons ~

What is Your Mission?

Life Lesson: There is great joy both in receiving God's gift of salvation and in offering His gift to others.

"Our life is not a 'mission trip,' our life is a mission." I was challenged when I heard these words. After His resurrection, Jesus appeared to the disciples and said to them, *"Peace be with you. As the Father has sent me, even so I am sending you."* John 20:21 (ESV) Jesus, sent by Father God to fulfill the justice required for the forgiveness of sin, now sends His disciples. In **Matthew 28:19 (ESV),** He gives this command, *"Go therefore and make disciples of all nations, baptizing them in the name of the Father and of the Son and of the Holy Spirit."* Just as the disciples, we are called to go. Often, we feel totally inadequate when faced with such a mission. God only asks that we obey His call.

A few years ago, I was leading a Bible Study and on the second week a young woman walked into the class. She was very timid and rarely looked up. She was listening intently but never spoke. As the class concluded and everyone was leaving, I knew that God was directing me to speak with her. Trusting the Holy Spirit to guide me, I sat down, and we talked.

She told me that she came to the United States as an adult from a middle eastern country. She shared that she had been seeking God all her life, but she felt unworthy of His love. She struggled to believe that God could forgive her. As I shared scriptures and my testimony, she eagerly listened. She readily acknowledged that she was a sinner as the scriptures stated in **Romans 3:23 *For everyone has sinned; we all fall short of God's glorious standard.*** When we read **Romans 6:23** she was amazed that God would offer salvation as a free gift. ***For the wages of sin is death, but the free gift of God is eternal life through Christ Jesus our Lord.*** In **Romans 5:8,** for the first time she heard the good news that even though she was a sinner, Jesus Christ died to pay the penalty for her sin. ***But God showed his great love for us by sending Christ to die for us while we were still sinners.*** **Romans 10:9-10** revealed to her that sincerely believing in Jesus and confessing Him as Lord results in a relationship with God. ***If you openly declare that Jesus is Lord and believe in your heart that God raised him from the dead, you will be saved. For it is by believing in your heart that you are made right with God, and it is by openly declaring your faith that you are saved.*** Then in **1 John 1:9** she listened intently as I read that God is faithful and just to not only forgive our sin but to make us righteous in His eyes. ***But if we confess our sins to him, he is faithful and just to forgive us our sins and to cleanse us from all wickedness.***

She looked at me and said, "It seems so simple." I said, "Yes, it is. All that you must do is believe Jesus died for you and receive Him as Savior." I was ready to invite her to pray when she looked at me straight in the eyes and said, "I receive Jesus as my Savior."

I was a bit shocked and said, "You do?!" She said, "Yes, I receive Jesus as my Savior!"

The joy of seeing someone receive the gift of salvation is beyond words. Her countenance changed. She was smiling and joyful. I told her to share her experience with her husband and we talked about baptism. As she continued and completed the Bible Study and it was evident that in Christ, she was indeed a 'new creation.' **Therefore, if anyone is in Christ, he is a new creation. The old has passed away; behold, the new has come. 2 Corinthians 5:17** She was experiencing the peace, hope and joy of being a part of God's family.

I communicated with her for a while and was encouraged that she was continuing her walk with God. Now two years later, God brought her to my mind. I wrote her name on my prayer list and prayed that she would continue to grow in her faith. After a couple of weeks, I got a phone call and, on the screen, I saw her name! She called because she wanted to be baptized. It was my privilege and joy to witness her baptism. Tears flooded my eyes as I watched her emerge from the baptismal waters. She had believed, received and obeyed God and is now eager to learn more about her new life in Jesus Christ.

What a privilege to experience the joy of sharing God's gospel. But what if I had not responded to the prompting of the Holy Spirit that day? What if I had not accepted my mission? God only knows how He will use that one life to grow His Kingdom. I think back at my own salvation experience and thank God that my coworker accepted her mission to share the gospel with me and my husband. Perhaps someone who reads this will believe and receive the gift of salvation. Just as we receive gifts from others that we may not deserve, God offers the free gift of salvation. We don't deserve it and we cannot earn it by trying to be good enough. **God saved you by his grace when you believed. And you can't take credit for this; it is a gift from God. Salvation is not a reward for the good things we have done, so none of us can boast about it.** Ephesians 2:8-9

The passage continues in verse 10, **For we are God's masterpiece. He has created us anew in Christ Jesus, so we can do the good things he planned for us long ago.** Every day there are those we encounter who are searching for peace. As God brings the opportunity, we are called to share the gospel in the power of the Holy Spirit and leave the results to God. As we share, we must not omit the most important part - the invitation. That day I found that sharing God's word was like bringing a cool cup of water to a person dying of thirst. All I had to do was offer it and it was eagerly received.

God has given us a mission. Go, share His good news.

But my life is worth nothing to me unless I use it for finishing the work assigned me by the Lord Jesus—the work of telling others the Good News about the wonderful grace of God.
Acts 20:24 (NLT)

~ Illuminating Life Lessons ~

~ Illuminating Life Lessons ~

~ Illuminating Life Lessons ~

Companion Books by Carol Graves

Three previous **fully in focus** books pictured above each with 52 attributes of God

Four Steps to Peace – the Journey
Bible Study focusing on Prayer

Let's Pray Together
Prayer journal

Children's books
My First Glimpse of God
The Shining Star of Christmas
The Grumble Bug
The Girl Who Wanted a Friend
The Boy Who Said, "I Can't!"

Shop for all books on facebook at
Carol Graves - Fully in Focus
e-mail: fullyinfocus@yahoo.com

www.ingramcontent.com/pod-product-compliance
Lightning Source LLC
Chambersburg PA
CBHW031256110426
42743CB00039B/286